Focus on PRONUNCIATION 2

THIRD EDITION

Linda Lane
American Language Program
Columbia University

Focus on Pronunciation 2, Third Edition

Copyright © 2013, 2005 by Pearson Education, Inc.
All rights reserved.

Pearson Education, 10 Bank Street, White Plains, NY 10606

Staff credits: The people who made up the *Focus on Pronunciation 2, Third Edition* team, representing editorial, production, design, and manufacturing, are Kim Casey, Dave Dickey, Ann France, Shelley Gazes, Maria Pia Marrella, Lise Minovitz, Liza Pleva, Mary Perrotta Rich, and Lynn Sobotta.

Cover image: Shutterstock.com
Text composition: ElectraGraphics, Inc.
Text font: 10/12 New Aster
Illustrations: Gary Torrisi and Jill Wood

Library of Congress Cataloging-in-Publication Data

Lane, Linda (Linda L.)
   Focus on pronunciation : [v.] 1 / Linda Lane. — 3rd ed.
        p. cm.
   ISBN 0-13-231493-2 (v. 1) — ISBN 0-13-231494-0 (v. 2) — ISBN 0-13-231500-9 (v. 3)   1.   English language—Pronunciation—Problems, exercises, etc.   2.   English language—Textbooks for foreign speakers.   I. Title.
   PE1137.L22 2012
   428.3'4—dc23

                                                                                        2011047246

ISBN 10: 0-13-231494-0
ISBN 13: 978-0-13-231494-7

Printed in the United States of America

2 3 4 5 6 7 8 9 10—V011—17 16 15 14 13

CONTENTS

INTRODUCTION

Focus on Pronunciation 2 is a comprehensive course that helps intermediate students speak English more clearly, confidently, and accurately. The course covers important topics from all aspects of pronunciation—sounds, stress, rhythm, and intonation.

The vowel and consonant sounds presented are those that occur frequently in English and that students recognize as new or difficult. Stress, rhythm, or intonation topics focus on pronunciation features that are important for clear English communication and that students can easily notice.

Each unit ends with Communication Practice about a theme (for example, celebrations or smart animals). As such, the activities and practice provide students with opportunities to improve their pronunciation and communication skills in context.

ORGANIZATION OF *FOCUS ON PRONUNCIATION 2*

Focus on Pronunciation 2 is divided into four parts: Vowels; Consonants; Stress in Words; and Rhythm and Intonation. Each unit deals with specific pronunciation points and has the following organization:

STEP 1 PRESENTATION

This section introduces, explains, and provides information about the pronunciation point. It may show how sounds are made or present other useful information. This is often achieved through the use of diagrams or illustrations. Pronunciation explanations are student friendly and easy to understand.

STEP 2 FOCUSED PRACTICE

This section consists of controlled classroom activities that allow students to develop skill and proficiency with the pronunciation point.

STEP 3 COMMUNICATION PRACTICE

This section provides communicative practice activities that focus on a theme. The activities are more open-ended and they ensure student involvement through the use of games and interactive tasks. When students are engaged in the communicative activities, they should be encouraged to keep in mind these global features of clear speaking:

- Speak slowly.
- Speak loudly enough.
- Pay attention to the ends of words.
- Use your voice to speak expressively.

NEW! NATURAL ENGLISH

New to this edition, the Natural English box in each unit highlights ways to speak English more naturally. In some cases, the Natural English box reviews or "pulls in" another important aspect of pronunciation that is not the focus of the current unit. Students might, for example, be reminded to group words together in a consonant or vowel unit in order to make their English more understandable to others. Additionally, the Natural English box may highlight the pronunciation of useful expressions (such as the use of *me too* for agreement).

This section consists of recorded homework activities. Accuracy Practice reviews key controlled exercises within the unit and serves as a warm-up for Fluency Practice, a freer speaking task that deals with the content of the unit. Students who have access to a computer can record their voices and review their pronunciation. The teacher can also listen to these recordings and provide feedback. Directions for how to make and send electronic files are at the back of the Student Book.

AUDIO PROGRAM

The **Classroom Audio CDs** have the recordings for all the pronunciation and listening exercises in the Student Book.

The **Student Audio CD-ROM** in the back of the book has all the recordings needed to complete the Accuracy Practice exercises in MP3 format.

KEY TO ICONS

🎧 —material recorded as part of the Classroom Audio CDs

🎧 —material recorded as part of the Student Audio CD-ROM in the Student Book

🎤 —material for students to record and give to the teacher

PLANNING A SYLLABUS

The units in *Focus on Pronunciation 2* can be used in any order. Teachers can "skip around"—for example, teaching the overview unit for Vowels, then a specific vowel unit, then the overview for Stress in Words, then a specific unit dealing with stress, and so on. Teachers who adopt this approach could also cover all the overview units at the beginning of the course and then skip around within the sections. The units can also be taught in order, first covering vowels, then consonants, and so on.

GENERAL REFERENCES

Most students have difficulty with English vowels and with stress, rhythm, and intonation, regardless of their native language background. With the exception of a few consonants (for example, the first sound in *think*), consonant difficulty depends more on the native language. The following references provide information on pronunciation problems related to native language:

Avery, Peter and S. Ehrlich. *Teaching American English Pronunciation*. Oxford: Oxford University Press, 1992.

Lane, Linda. *Tips for Teaching Pronunciation*. Pearson Longman, 2010.

Swan, M. and Smith, B. *Learner English, 2nd Ed.* Cambridge, UK: Cambridge University Press, 2001.

The following research influenced the content and approach of this book:

Avery, Peter and S. Ehrlich. *Teaching American English Pronunciation*. Oxford: Oxford University Press, 1992.

Celce-Murcia, Marianne, D. M. Brinton and J. M. Goodwin. *Teaching Pronunciation: A Reference for Teachers of English to Speakers of Other Languages*. Cambridge: Cambridge University Press, 1996.

Lane, Linda. *Tips for Teaching Pronunciation*. Pearson Longman, 2010.

ABOUT THE AUTHOR

Linda Lane is a senior faculty member in the American Language Program of Columbia University. In addition to the *Focus on Pronunciation* series, she is also the author of *Tips for Teaching Pronunciation,* Pearson, 2010. She served as director of the Columbia University Humanities Media Center for 10 years and coordinated Columbia's TESOL Certificate Program for another 10 years, teaching classes in Applied Phonetics and Pronunciation Teaching and Introduction to Second Language Acquisition. She received her EdD in Applied Linguistics from Teachers College, Columbia University, her MA in Linguistics from Yale University, and her BS in Mathematics from the University of Washington, Seattle.

ACKNOWLEDGMENTS

I am indebted to a number of people whose support, patience, and good humor made this book possible. I am grateful for the help and suggestions of my editors at Pearson: Lise Minovitz, Lynn Sobotta, and Kim Casey.

I would like to thank the reviewers who offered suggestions that shaped the new edition: Ashkhen Strack, Tunxis Community College, Farmington, CT; Victor Matthews, Assumption College, Lampang, Thailand; Judy Gilbert, Columbia University, New York, NY; Joanna Ghosh, University of Pennsylvania, Philadelphia, PA.

In addition, I would like to thank those reviewers whose insights shaped the previous edition: Dr. John Milbury-Steen, Temple University, Philadelphia, PA; Michele McMenamin, Rutgers University, Piscataway, NJ; Gwendolyn Kane, Rutgers University, Piscataway, NJ; William Crawford, Georgetown University, Washington, D.C.; Linda Wells, University of Washington, Seattle, WA; Tara Narcross, Columbus State Community College, Columbus, OH; Robert Baldwin, UCLA, Los Angeles, CA; Mary Di Stefano Diaz, Broward Community College, Davie, FL; Barbara Smith-Palinkas, University of South Florida, Tampa, FL; Susan Jamieson, Bellevue Community College, Bellevue, WA; Andrea Toth, City College of San Francisco, San Francisco, CA; Fernando Barboza, ICPNA, Lima, Peru; Adrianne P. Ochoa, Georgia State University, Atlanta, GA; Greg Jewell, Drexel University, Philadelphia, PA; Cindy Chang, University of Washington, Seattle, WA; Emily Rosales, Université du Québec à Montréal/École de Langues, Montréal, QC, Canada.

My colleagues at the American Language Program at Columbia University have always been an inspiration and source of generous support.

For the encouragement and patience of my family, Mile, Martha, Sonia, and Luke, and of my dear friend Mary Jerome, whom I miss every day, I am also deeply grateful.

Finally, I want to thank my students—for teaching me how they learn pronunciation, for wanting to improve their pronunciation, and for showing me how to help them.

–Linda Lane

VOWELS

UNIT	PRONUNCIATION FOCUS	COMMUNICATION PRACTICE
1	Vowel Overview	Watching Video
2	/iy/ sh<u>ee</u>p and /ɪ/ sh<u>i</u>p	Snow and Sand
3	/ey/ l<u>a</u>te, /ɛ/ l<u>e</u>t, and /ɪ/ l<u>i</u>t	A New Year
4	/æ/ bl<u>a</u>ck and /ɛ/ r<u>e</u>d	Superstitions
5	/ə/ c<u>u</u>p	Love and Marriage
6	/ɑ/ c<u>o</u>p and /ə/ c<u>u</u>p	Luck and Chance
7	Review: /ɛ/ n<u>e</u>t, /æ/ N<u>a</u>t, /ə/ n<u>u</u>t, and /ɑ/ n<u>o</u>t	Happiness
8	/r/ after Vowels	World Records
9	/ow/ b<u>oa</u>t, /ɑ/ p<u>o</u>t, and /ɔ/ b<u>ough</u>t	Home
10	/uw/ f<u>oo</u>d and /ʊ/ b<u>oo</u>k	Dilemmas

Vowel Overview

A | *There are eleven vowels and three complex vowels in English. Listen.*

		Front	**Central**	**Back**
High	Tense	/iy/ heat		/uw/ tooth
	Relaxed	/ɪ/ hit		/ʊ/ took
Mid	Tense	/ey/ hate	/ə/ cut	/ow/ coat
	Relaxed	/ɛ/ head		
Low		/æ/ hat		/ɔ/ caught
			/ɑ/ hot	

B | *Look at the diagram. Different positions of the tongue create different vowel sounds. For example, when you say the vowel in* hot, *your tongue is low, in the center of your mouth.*

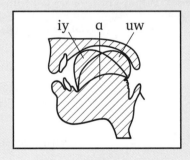

There are three complex vowels, called diphthongs. *Listen.*

/ay/	**/aw/**	**/oy/**
eye	how	boy

EXERCISE 1: Seeing and Feeling Vowels

A | *Listen and repeat the words.*

1. hot, heat

2. tea, too

3. day, do

B | *PAIRS: Say the following word combinations slowly. Your partner will describe your lips and mouth as you change from word to word. (You can also do this by yourself with a mirror.)*

1. *hot-heat-hot-heat* (What happens as you go from *hot* to *heat*?)

2. *tea-too-tea-too* (What happens as you go from *tea* to *too*?)

3. *day-do-day-do* (What happens as you go from *day* to *do*?)

EXERCISE 2: Hearing the Ends of Vowels

The vowels /iy/, /ey/, /uw/, and /ow/ end in a short /y/ or /w/ sound, called a *glide*. The glide is not always shown in the spelling of a word. When another vowel follows /iy/, /ey/, /uw/, or /ow/, use the glide to join the two vowels.

Listen and repeat. Join words together.

/iy/	/ey/	/uw/	/ow/
1. see^{y} us	3. say it	5. do^{w} it	7. go^{w} up
2. be^{y} over	4. pay Ann	6. too^{w} easy	8. show us

EXERCISE 3: Tense and Relaxed Vowels

A | *Listen and repeat the words. Use the mouth pictures to help you pronounce the vowels.*

Tense Vowels   **Relaxed Vowels**

1. sheep /iy/   4. ship /ɪ/

2. paper /ey/   5. pepper /ɛ/

3. Luke /uw/   6. look /ʊ/

B | *Look at the pictures of the tense and relaxed vowels in Part A. Complete the sentences with the correct words.*

1. When you say the tense vowel /iy/, your lips are _____ (spread/relaxed).

2. When you say /ɪ/, your lips are _____ (spread/relaxed).

3. Your lips are _____ (more/less) rounded for /uw/ than for /ʊ/.

EXERCISE 4: Listen for Differences: Vowels

A | *Listen and repeat the words.*

1.	**a.** seen	**5.**	**a.** pool	**9.**	**a.** daily
	b. sin		**b.** pull		**b.** deli
2.	**a.** Luke	**6.**	**a.** taste	**10.**	**a.** each
	b. look		**b.** test		**b.** itch
3.	**a.** wait	**7.**	**a.** sheep	**11.**	**a.** who'd
	b. wet		**b.** ship		**b.** hood
4.	**a.** late	**8.**	**a.** reason	**12.**	**a.** leave
	b. let		**b.** risen		**b.** live

B | *Listen again and circle the words you hear.*

EXERCISE 5: Dictations

PAIRS: Read a sentence to your partner (but don't show it to your partner). Your partner will write what you say. Then switch roles. Student A's sentences are on page 201. Student B's sentences are on page 205.

EXAMPLE:

STUDENT A says: How do you spell *ship*?

STUDENT B writes: How do you spell *ship*?

WATCHING VIDEO

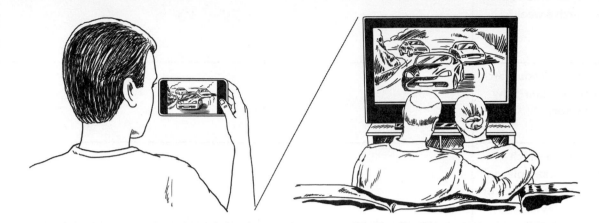

EXERCISE 6: Video Content

A | *Listen to the words and phrases.*

sh<u>o</u>pping shows	dr<u>a</u>mas	adventure m<u>o</u>vies	c<u>o</u>medies
tr<u>a</u>vel shows	cl<u>a</u>ssic movies	qu<u>i</u>z shows	online amateur[1] v<u>i</u>deos
f<u>oo</u>d shows	m<u>y</u>steries	cart<u>oo</u>ns	news shows
b<u>u</u>siness reports	<u>a</u>ction movies	t<u>a</u>lent shows	t<u>a</u>lk shows

---

Natural English

Two vowel sounds together in a word are usually joined with a /y/ or /w/ sound. The /y/ or /w/ sound is rarely written.

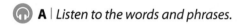

vide^yo, radi^yo, the^yaters

In words such as *people* or *piece*, the rule does not apply because the two vowel letters represent only one vowel sound.

B | *The underlined letters in Part A have /ɪ/, /uw/, /ɑ/, or /æ/ sounds. Write each word or phrase from the box in the correct column below.*

/ɪ/ h<u>i</u>t	/uw/ t<u>oo</u>th	/ɑ/ h<u>o</u>t	/æ/ h<u>a</u>t
		shopping shows	

---

[1] amateur: *someone who does something because he or she enjoys it, but not for money*

EXERCISE 7: Your Turn

GROUPS: Read the questions in the chart. Then write your answers and share them with your classmates.

How much video do you watch a week?	
Do you think you watch too much video? Why or why not?	
How do you watch video (for example, on a TV set, a computer, or a mobile device)?	
What kinds of video do you watch?	

STEP 4   EXTENDED PRACTICE

🎧🎙 **Accuracy Practice** *Listen again to Exercise 4A on page 4. Then record the words.*

🎙 **Fluency Practice** *Record the questions and answers from the chart in Exercise 7.*

UNIT 2 /iy/ sh**ee**p and /ɪ/ sh**i**p

The pictures show how to say /iy/ and /ɪ/.

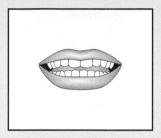 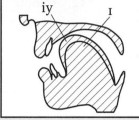 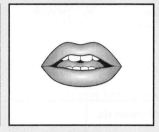

shee**p, l**ea**ve /iy/**

Spread your lips.
/iy/ ends with a /y/ sound.

shi**p, l**i**ve /ɪ/**

Relax your lips.
Lower your tongue a little.

Notes

1. When /iy/ is followed by another vowel, use /y/ to join the two vowels.

    radi^yo   see^ya movie

2. Many languages have a vowel similar to the vowel in *sheep*.
3. The vowel in *ship* is a new vowel for many students.

Spellings for /iy/	Spellings for /ɪ/
Common *ee* f**ee**t, succ**ee**d, s**ee** *ie* bel**ie**ve, p**ie**ce, rel**ie**f *ei* rec**ei**ve *ea* **ea**st, **ea**t, m**ea**n *i* mach**i**ne, pol**i**ce, sk**i**	**Common** *i* (between consonants): g**i**ve, s**i**t, l**i**sten
Other *e* k**e**y, m**e**dium, p**eo**ple	**Other** *u* b**u**siness, b**u**sy *ui* b**ui**ld, g**ui**lty *y* g**y**m
	Unusual *o* w**o**men

7

STEP 2 FOCUSED PRACTICE

EXERCISE 1: Words with /iy/ and /ɪ/

🎧 *Listen and repeat the words.*

	/iy/				/ɪ/		
1.	ski	**5.**	beach	**9.**	ship	**13.**	busy
2.	sheep	**6.**	leave	**10.**	middle	**14.**	women
3.	believe	**7.**	reason	**11.**	live	**15.**	kick
4.	machine	**8.**	people	**12.**	minute	**16.**	miss

EXERCISE 2: Listen for Differences: /iy/ vs. /ɪ/

🎧 **A** | *Listen and repeat the words.*

1.	**a.**	eat	**3.**	**a.**	heel	**5.**	**a.**	reason	**7.**	**a.**	deed
	b.	it		**b.**	hill		**b.**	risen		**b.**	did
2.	**a.**	steal	**4.**	**a.**	sheep	**6.**	**a.**	leave	**8.**	**a.**	each
	b.	still		**b.**	ship		**b.**	live		**b.**	itch

🎧 **B** | *Listen again and circle the words you hear.*

EXERCISE 3: Bingo

🎧 **A** | *Listen and repeat the words on the Bingo card.*

1. reason	**5.** ship	**9.** live	**13.** heel
2. it	**6.** each	**10.** fit	**14.** sheep
3. hill	**7.** risen	**11.** rich	**15.** leave
4. itch	**8.** feet	**12.** reach	**16.** eat

🎧 **B** | *Now play Bingo. Use the card in Part A. Listen carefully and cross out each word you hear. When you've crossed out a complete row or column ⊞ ⊞, say "Bingo!"*

EXERCISE 4: Differences in Meaning

PAIRS: Ask your partner to define one of the words in the left column. Pronounce the vowel carefully so your partner knows which definition to read to you.

EXAMPLE:

STUDENT A: What does *leave* mean?

STUDENT B: *Leave* means "the opposite of *stay*."

	Words	Definitions
1. a.	leave	the opposite of *stay*
b.	live	the opposite of *die*
2. a.	rich	wealthy
b.	reach	to extend the arm to get something
3. a.	ship	a large boat
b.	sheep	a woolly animal
4. a.	fill	to put things in a container
b.	feel	to touch something

EXERCISE 5: Joining Vowels Together: /iy/ + another vowel

Listen and repeat the words and phrases. Use /y/ to join the vowels together. The letter y has been added to help you say the words correctly.

1. be^y a doctor
2. ide^{y}a
3. medi^{y}um
4. pi^{y}ano
5. radi^{y}o
6. rainy afternoon
7. re^{y}alize
8. see^{y}it
9. seri^{y}ous

EXERCISE 6: Sentences Full of Sounds

A | *Listen and repeat the sentences.*

1. On the weekend, the women went swimming in the deep river.
2. We found Miss Meese's mittens on the table after the meeting.
3. Steven Stivens reached for a dish of rich ice cream.
4. Sit in this seat and draw a picture of a sheep and a ship.
5. Does the criminal still steal political secrets?

B | *GROUPS: Choose a sentence and say it to your classmates.*

SNOW AND SAND

EXERCISE 7: What Will They Miss?

Steve Stimson is from Boulder, Colorado. He's leaving home to go to college in Miami, Florida. Silvia Seely is from Miami. She's decided to go to college in Boulder. They both love their hometowns, but they want to live in another part of the country for a while. They know they're going to miss their hometowns.

A | *Listen and repeat the words and phrases. The bold letters are pronounced /iy/ or /ɪ/.*

1. sk**ii**ng
2. the b**ea**ch
3. Cuban cuis**i**ne
4. snowboarding

5. mounta**i**ns
6. palm tr**ee**s
7. s**i**tting in front of a fire
8. the change of s**ea**sons

9. snow
10. fresh s**ea**food
11. sw**i**mming
12. w**i**nter

B | *What will Steve and Silvia miss when they go to college? Write each word and phrase from Part A in the correct column.*

Steve will miss . . .   **Silvia will miss . . .**

skiing

_____   _____

_____   _____

_____   _____

_____   _____

_____   _____

C | *Check your answers with a partner. Then use the words and phrases to make sentences about Steve and Silvia. Follow the examples.*

EXAMPLES:

Steve's from Boulder. He'll miss the change of seasons.

Silvia's from Miami. She'll miss the beach.

EXERCISE 8: Your Turn

Find two students who have had to leave their hometowns or countries. Ask them what they miss. Write their names and what they miss on a piece of paper. Follow the example.

EXAMPLE:

Mai misses Korean food.

> **Natural English**
>
> Use the contraction of *will* after pronouns. Contractions make your English sound more natural.
>
> > *He'll* miss winter.
> >
> > *She'll* miss swimming.

STEP 4 EXTENDED PRACTICE

Accuracy Practice *Listen again to Exercises 1 and 2A on page 8. Then record the words.*

Fluency Practice *In general, people spend more vacation time at beaches than at ski resorts. Which do you like better? Why? Record your answers.*

/ey/ l<u>a</u>te, /ɛ/ l<u>e</u>t, and /ɪ/ l<u>i</u>t

STEP 1 PRESENTATION

The pictures show how to say /ey/, /ɛ/, and /ɪ/.

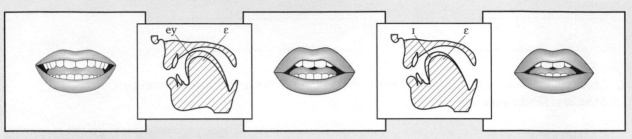

l<u>a</u>te, p<u>ai</u>n /ey/

Spread your lips.
/ey/ ends with a
/y/ sound.

l<u>e</u>t, p<u>e</u>n /ɛ/

Don't spread your lips
too much. Your mouth
is more relaxed for /ɛ/
than for /ey/.

l<u>i</u>t, p<u>i</u>n /ɪ/

Don't spread your lips.
Your mouth is more
closed for /ɪ/ than for /ɛ/.

Spellings for /ey/	Spellings for /ɛ/

Common
aC(C)e (C is a consonant; *e* is silent)
  f**a**ce, n**a**me, t**a**ste
ai r**ai**n, w**ai**t
ay d**ay**, pl**ay**
	Common
	eC(C) (C is a consonant)
	  b**e**st, g**e**t, l**e**t
	ead br**ead**, h**ead**, inst**ead**

Other *ei* **ei**ght, n**ei**ghbor *ey* conv**ey**,[1] th**ey** *ea* br**ea**k, gr**ea**t	**Other** *ai* ag**ai**n, ag**ai**nst, s**ai**d *ea* br**ea**kfast, h**ea**vy, w**ea**ther
Spellings for /ɪ/: See Unit 2.	

---

[1] convey: *to communicate a message with or without using words*

STEP 2 FOCUSED PRACTICE

EXERCISE 1: Words with /ey/ and /ɛ/

Listen and repeat the words.

/ey/				/ɛ/			
1.	late	5.	occasion	9.	let	13.	guess
2.	age	6.	afraid	10.	healthy	14.	breakfast
3.	break	7.	name	11.	festival[1]	15.	wedding
4.	celebration	8.	weight	12.	said	16.	friend

EXERCISE 2: Listen for Differences: /ey/ vs. /ɛ/ vs. /ɪ/

A | *Listen and repeat the words.*

1. a. mate
   b. met
   c. mitt

2. a. pain
   b. pen
   c. pin

3. a. late
   b. let
   c. lit

4. a. sail
   b. sell
   c. sill

5. a. H
   b. etch[2]
   c. itch

6. a. takes
   b. Tex
   c. ticks

B | *Listen again and circle the words you hear.*

C | *PAIRS: Choose a word from Part A and ask your partner how to spell it. Be sure to pronounce the vowel carefully.*

EXAMPLE:

STUDENT A: How do you spell *mitt*?

STUDENT B: M-I-T-T.

---

[1] festival: *a special occasion when people celebrate something;* [2] etch: *to cut designs into metal or glass*

EXERCISE 3: Bingo

🎧 **A** | *Listen and repeat the words on the Bingo card.*

1. pain	**5.** edge	**9.** sailor[1]	**13.** mitt	**17.** pen
2. met	**6.** fill	**10.** pin	**14.** fell	**18.** wet
3. lit	**7.** wait	**11.** hid	**15.** let	**19.** mate
4. age	**8.** late	**12.** fail	**16.** head	**20.** seller

🎧 **B** | *Now play Bingo. Use the card in Part A. Listen carefully and cross out each word you hear. When you've crossed out a complete row or column* *, say "Bingo!"*

EXERCISE 4: Sounds and Spellings

🎧 **A** | *Listen and repeat the words. The bold letters are pronounced /ey/, /ɛ/ or /ɪ/.*

1. br**ea**k
2. br**ea**d
3. b**ee**n
4. r**ai**n
5. ag**ai**n
6. pr**e**tty
7. d**ay**
8. s**ay**s
9. m**a**ny

B | *Circle the words in Part A with /ey/ pronunciations. Underline the words with /ɛ/ pronunciations. The remaining words have /ɪ/ pronunciations. Then compare your answers with the class.*

EXERCISE 5: Sentences Full of Sounds

🎧 **A** | *Listen and repeat the sentences.*

1. The **rai**n wr**e**cked the r**a**ke that R**i**ck l**e**ft on the r**oa**d.

2. T**e**x is t**a**king t**i**cks out of T**e**ssie's t**a**me t**e**rrier.

3. How l**a**te will you l**e**t me keep the light l**i**t?

4. The man with the m**i**tt m**e**t the first m**a**te.

B | *Choose a sentence. Say it to the class.*

---

[1] sailor: *someone who works on a ship*

A NEW YEAR

EXERCISE 6: New Year's Resolutions

For many people, the New Year starts on January 1. It's a time for a fresh start. People make resolutions, or promises, to improve their financial situation, their health, or their personal lives.

🎧 *Listen to these New Year's resolutions and write them in the blanks. Then compare your answers with a partner.*

I'm going to . . .*

1. _____ save _____ money _____
2. _____ _____
3. _____ _____

   _____
4. _____ _____
5. _____ more _____
6. _____ _____ _____ with my

   _____ and _____
7. _____ _____
8. _____ _____
9. _____ a _____ _____
10. _____ _____

> ***Natural English**
>
> When *going to* is used as a future verb, it's often pronounced *gonna*. If you use this pronunciation, don't add *to* after *gonna*.
>
> I'm *gonna* save money.
>
> I'm *gonna* watch less TV.

EXERCISE 7: Holi, the Festival of Colors

A | *Listen and repeat. The bold letters are pronounced /ɛ/ or /ɪ/. Make sure you understand the words.*

lunar calendar	water **pi**stols
v**i**ctory	powders
evil	l**ea**d and mercury[1]
ball**oo**ns	scrub

B | *Listen to the recording and then answer the questions with a partner.*

1. Where is Holi celebrated?
2. When is Holi celebrated?
3. How do people celebrate Holi?
4. Do you know of any celebrations that are similar to Holi?

STEP 4 EXTENDED PRACTICE

Accuracy Practice *Listen again to Exercises 1 and 2A on page 13. Then record the words.*

Fluency Practice *Record your answers to the questions.*

Do you make New Year's resolutions? If so, what are they?

---

[1] lead and mercury: *elements that can be harmful to health, especially to children*

UNIT 4 /æ/ bl<u>a</u>ck and /ɛ/ r<u>e</u>d

The pictures show how to say /æ/ and /ɛ/.

bl<u>a</u>ck, s<u>a</u>d /æ/

r<u>e</u>d, s<u>ai</u>d /ɛ/

Open your mouth and spread your lips.
The tip of your tongue is behind your bottom teeth.

Your mouth is more closed for /ɛ/ than for /æ/.

Spellings for /æ/	Spellings for /ɛ/
Common *aC(C)* (*C* is a consonant) h<u>a</u>t, gl<u>a</u>d, h<u>a</u>nd	See Unit 3.
Other *au* l<u>au</u>gh *ai* pl<u>ai</u>d	

STEP 2 FOCUSED PRACTICE

EXERCISE 1: Words with /æ/

🎧 *Listen and repeat the words.*

1. black
2. relax
3. bad

4. matter
5. answer
6. happen

7. magic
8. exactly
9. path

EXERCISE 2: Listen for Differences: /æ/ vs. /ɛ/

🎧 **A** | *Listen and repeat the words.*

1. **a.** bath
   b. Beth

2. **a.** past
   b. pest

3. **a.** laughed
   b. left

4. **a.** sat
   b. set

5. **a.** gas
   b. guess

6. **a.** bad
   b. bed

7. **a.** axe
   b. X

8. **a.** sad
   b. said

🎧 **B** | *Listen again and circle the words you hear.*

C | *PAIRS: Say a word from Part A. Your partner will tell you which word you said.*

EXERCISE 3: Differences in Meaning

🎧 **A** | *Listen to the sentences and responses.*

Sentences	Responses
1. **a.** That's an unusual <u>X</u>. **b.** That's an unusual <u>axe</u>.	Yes, it looks more like a *W*. It's from my collection of old tools.
2. **a.** After I told him the story, he <u>laughed</u>. **b.** After I told him the story, he <u>left</u>.	It was a very funny story. He had a doctor's appointment.
3. **a.** I need a <u>tan</u>. **b.** I need a <u>ten</u>.	I think you look just fine. Well, don't ask me—you still owe me twenty dollars from last week!
4. **a.** My <u>pan</u> is no good. **b.** My <u>pen</u> is no good.	Another excuse not to cook! Another excuse not to write that letter!

B | *PAIRS: Choose a sentence from Part A. Pronounce the underlined word carefully so your partner can say the correct response.*

SUPERSTITIONS

EXERCISE 4: Superstitious Beliefs

A | *Listen and repeat. Make sure you understand the words.*

rabbit	ensures	wedding	bouquet	spirit	anthropologists

B | *Read the situations below. The bold letters are pronounced /æ/ or /ɛ/. Each situation is associated with a superstitious belief.*

_____ **1.** a bl**a**ck c**a**t crossing your p**a**th

_____ **2.** carrying a r**a**bbit's foot

_____ **3.** breaking a mirror

_____ **4.** knocking on wood

_____ **5.** walking under a l**a**dder

_____ **6.** finding a four-leaf clover

_____ **7.** throwing salt over your l**e**ft shoulder

_____ **8.** carrying a baby upstairs

_____ **9.** the bride and groom seeing each other before the w**e**dding c**e**remony

_____ **10.** wearing garlic around your n**e**ck

_____ **11.** throwing the w**e**dding bouquet

_____ **12.** throwing rice at the couple **a**fter the w**e**dding

(continued on next page)

_____ **13.** opening the doors and windows **a**fter a person's d**ea**th

_____ **14.** a howling dog

_____ **15.** finding a p**e**nny

_____ **16.** the number 13

_____ **17.** the number 4

_____ **18.** Friday the 13th

C | _Listen to the recording. Check (✓) the situations you hear. Do these situations include good luck, bad luck, or neither? (You can check your answers below.) Do any of the situations make sense?_

---

*Natural English

Use *make sénse* to say that something is logical and understandable. *Make* is usually less heavily stressed than the direct object, *sense*.

> Walking under a ladder is bad luck? That superstition *makes sénse*—the ladder could fall.

Use *doesn't (don't) make sense* to say that something isn't logical or understandable.

> Black cats bring bad luck? That *doesn't make sense*. I have a black cat, and I don't have bad luck.

EXERCISE 5: Your Turn

GROUPS: Discuss the questions.

1. Are you a superstitious person? Explain.
2. What superstitions are common in your country?

STEP 4 EXTENDED PRACTICE

Accuracy Practice _Listen again to Exercises 1 and 2A on page 18. Then record the words._

Fluency Practice _Record your answers to the questions in Exercise 5._

EXERCISE 4C: 1. Good luck: 2, 4, 6, 7, 8, 11, 12, 13, 15; **Bad luck:** 1, 3, 5, 9, 16, 17, 18; **Neither good luck or bad luck: 10:** Wearing garlic around your neck protects you from vampires; **14:** A howling dog means someone is going to die.

STEP 1 PRESENTATION

The picture shows how to say /ə/.

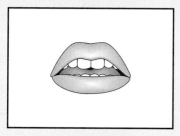

cu**p, m**o**ney /ə/**

Your mouth is almost closed.
Your tongue rests in the center of your mouth.

Notes

1. /ə/ is the most common vowel in English. It's the sound of most unstressed vowels.
2. The English "hesitation word" *uh* is the vowel /ə/.

The restaurant is . . . uh . . . uh . . . I think it's on State Street.

Spellings for /ə/	

Common
    u (between consonants)
        c**u**p, h**u**ngry, l**u**ck
	Same Spelling, Different Sounds
	    o m**o**nkey /ə/, d**o**nkey /ɑ/, d**o**ne /ə/
	        st**o**ne, al**o**ne /ow/
	    ou r**ou**gh /ə/ alth**ou**gh /ow/
	        thr**ou**gh /uw/ b**ou**ght /ɔ/
	    oo bl**oo**d /ə/ f**oo**d /uw/
	        g**oo**d /ʊ/

Other
    o s**o**me, m**o**ney, disc**o**ver
    ou t**ou**gh, c**ou**ntry, en**ou**gh
    oe d**oe**s, d**oe**sn't
    a wh**a**t, w**a**s
    oo bl**oo**d, fl**oo**d
	Different Spellings, Same Sound
	    o, u s**o**n, s**u**n /ə/
	    u, ou **u**s, jeal**ou**s /ə/

STEP 2 FOCUSED PRACTICE

EXERCISE 1: Words with /ə/

🎧 *Listen and repeat the words. Your mouth should be almost closed when you say /ə/.*

1. son	**4.** number	**7.** country	**10.** dull
2. once	**5.** wasn't	**8.** doesn't	**11.** money
3. love	**6.** thumb	**9.** cup	**12.** blood

EXERCISE 2: Phrases with /ə/

🎧 *Listen and repeat the phrases.*

1. a summer Sunday	**4.** my younger brother	**7.** does or doesn't
2. enough money	**5.** a sudden flood	**8.** funny stuff
3. a hungry buffalo	**6.** double trouble	**9.** a loving mother

EXERCISE 3: Sounds and Spelling

🎧 **A |** *Listen to the word pairs. Write **S** if the bold sounds are the same. Write **D** if the bold sounds are different.*

1. what, hat ___D___	**6.** tough, though _____
2. flood, foot _____	**7.** cut, company _____
3. country, count _____	**8.** one, won _____
4. sun, son _____	**9.** done, bone _____
5. luck, lock _____	**10.** rush, touch _____

B | *PAIRS: Choose two word pairs that are the same and two word pairs that are different. Say them to your partner.*

EXERCISE 4: Rhyme

🎧 **A |** *Listen to the rhyme. In sentence 3, the* h *of* he *is not pronounced and* was he *is pronounced exactly like* Wuzzy.

1. Fuzzy Wuzzy was a bear.
2. Fuzzy Wuzzy had no hair.
3. Fuzzy Wuzzy wasn't very fuzzy, was he?

B | *PAIRS: Read the rhyme. Join words together and speak smoothly. Take turns.*

EXERCISE 5: Unstressed Vowels

Most unstressed vowels are pronounced /ə/. They can be spelled with any vowel letter.

A | *Listen to the words. Notice how the underlined letters are pronounced.*

1. hápp<u>e</u>n
2. jéal<u>ou</u>s
3. p<u>o</u>líce
4. díst<u>a</u>nce
5. práct<u>i</u>ce
6. m<u>a</u>chíne
7. c<u>o</u>ntról
8. nát<u>io</u>n<u>a</u>l
9. d<u>e</u>vél<u>o</u>p

B | *The words below have been "respelled" to show how the unstressed vowel is pronounced. Listen to the words. Then write the correct spelling of the word in the blank.*

1. tədáy

   _____

2. əgó

   _____

3. póssəbəl

   _____

4. béautəfəl

   _____

5. lémən

   _____

6. əccúr

   _____

7. təníght

   _____

8. thóusənd

   _____

C | *PAIRS: Compare your answers. Then practice saying the words.*

EXERCISE 6: Conversations

A | *Listen to the recording and complete the sentences with the words you hear. The missing words have the /ə/ sound.*

1. **ALI:** What do you want for _____?

   LEILA: _____. I'm not _____.

2. **ALI:** How _____ _____ do you have?

   LEILA: Not even _____ to take the _____.

3. **ALI:** Why did your _____ call?

   LEILA: She's _____ next _____.

B | *PAIRS: Practice the conversations.*

LOVE AND MARRIAGE

EXERCISE 7: Phrases and Idioms with *Love*

A | *Listen to the recording and complete the sentences with the words you hear. The shaded phrases are idioms or expressions.*

Sentences	**Responses**
1. It was _____ at _____ _____ with Julian—we were only 14 when we met. My parents called it _____ _____.	**a.** There's no _____ _____ between those two, but I don't know why.
2. Angela said she wouldn't come to the party if her sister Lucy came.	**b.** It's a _____-_____ relationship. I think they should break up.
3. Mickey and his girlfriend always seem to be fighting.	**c.** And now, you and Julian are celebrating your tenth anniversary.
4. Why do you spend so much time on that old car?	**d.** It's a _____ of _____. I enjoy fixing it up.
5. Are you going to accept the job offer?	**e.** _____ for _____ _____ _____. I'd have to travel a lot. And I don't like traveling.

B | *PAIRS: Make conversations by matching the sentences and responses. Then practice them with a partner. Take turns.*

C | *What do you think the shaded idioms mean?*

EXERCISE 8: A Successful Marriage

A | *Listen and repeat the words. The bold letters are pronounced /ə/.*

c**ou**ple	l**o**ve	c**o**me fr**o**m	each **o**ther	tr**u**st	c**u**lture

B | *Read the sentences below. Check (✓) the three statements that you think are most important for a successful marriage.*

A married couple should . . .

_____ 1. be in love

_____ 2. be about the same age

_____ 3. like each other*

_____ 4. trust each other

_____ 5. come from the same social class

_____ 6. have the same economic background

_____ 7. have the same level of education

_____ 8. have the same racial backgrounds

_____ 9. have the same ethnic and cultural backgrounds

_____ 10. have the same religious beliefs

---

*Natural English

Pronounce *each óther* as one word, like *ea-chother*. Use *each other* with subjects that can refer to two or more people.

The couple should like each óther.

C | *GROUPS: Compare the answers you checked in Part B. Discuss your choices. What else is important for a successful marriage?*

STEP 4 EXTENDED PRACTICE

Accuracy Practice *Listen again to Exercises 2 and 3A on page 22. Then record the phrases and word pairs.*

Fluency Practice *Record the sentences you checked in Exercise 8B. Explain why you think they're important.*

UNIT 6 /ɑ/ cop and /ə/ cup

STEP 1 PRESENTATION

The pictures show how to say /ɑ/ and /ə/.

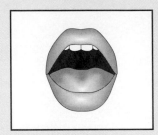

cop, lock /ɑ/

Your mouth is open.
Your tongue is low, in the
center of your mouth.

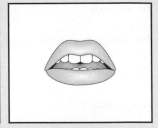

cup, luck /ə/

Your mouth is almost closed.
Your tongue is in the middle
of your mouth, neither high
nor low.

Spellings for /ɑ/	Spellings for /ə/
Common *o* (between consonants) c**o**p, l**o**ck, p**o**ssible	See Unit 5.
Other *a* c**a**r, f**a**ther, w**a**tch *ua* g**ua**rd	

STEP 2 FOCUSED PRACTICE

EXERCISE 1: Words with /ɑ/ and /ə/

🎧 *Listen and repeat the words. Your mouth should be open for /ɑ/. Your mouth should be almost closed for /ə/.*

	/ɑ/				/ə/		
1.	rob	6.	modern	11.	shut	16.	tough
2.	shot	7.	odds[1]	12.	stomach	17.	gun
3.	soccer	8.	block	13.	luck	18.	sudden
4.	lottery	9.	popular	14.	wonder	19.	mustard
5.	dock	10.	problem	15.	southern	20.	hundred

EXERCISE 2: Vowel Patterns

🎧 **A** | *Listen and repeat the phrases. The bold letters are pronounced /ɑ/ or /ə/.*

1. **o**dd n**u**mbers
2. l**u**cky l**o**ttery winner
3. not en**ou**gh
4. t**ou**gh j**o**b
5. st**o**p s**u**ddenly
6. modern c**ou**ntries
7. p**o**pular g**o**vernment
8. c**o**me **o**n
9. **u**nderd**o**g[2]
10. r**o**tten l**u**ck
11. **o**ne bl**o**ck
12. y**ou**ng father

B | *What are the vowel patterns of the phrases? Write each phrase in the correct column.*

/ɑ/ /ə/	/ə/ /ɑ/
odd numbers	_____
_____	_____
_____	_____
_____	_____
_____	_____
_____	_____

C | *PAIRS: Compare your answers. Then practice saying the phrases. Take turns.*

---

[1] odds: *how likely it is that something will or will not happen;* [2] underdog: *someone who is not expected to win*

EXERCISE 3: Listen for Differences: /ɑ/ vs. /ə/

🎧 **A** | *Listen and repeat the words.*

1.	**a.** wants	**5.**	**a.** collar	**9.**	**a.** lock
	b. once		**b.** color		**b.** luck
2.	**a.** box	**6.**	**a.** socks	**10.**	**a.** cop
	b. bucks		**b.** sucks		**b.** cup
3.	**a.** shot	**7.**	**a.** dock	**11.**	**a.** not
	b. shut		**b.** duck		**b.** nut
4.	**a.** rob	**8.**	**a.** hot	**12.**	**a.** blonder
	b. rub		**b.** hut		**b.** blunder[1]

🎧 **B** | *Listen again and circle the words you hear.*

EXERCISE 4: Differences in Meaning

🎧 **A** | *Listen to the questions and responses.*

	Questions	**Responses**
1.	**a.** What's a <u>dock</u>?	A dock is a place where boats can be tied up.
	b. What's a <u>duck</u>?	A duck is a water bird that makes a "quack-quack" sound.
2.	**a.** What's a <u>cup</u>?	A cup is a container for hot drinks.
	b. What's a <u>cop</u>?	A cop is a police officer.
3.	**a.** What's "<u>succor</u>"?	*Succor* is a formal word for *help*.
	b. What's <u>soccer</u>?	Soccer is the most popular sport in the world.
4.	**a.** What's a <u>knot</u>?	When you tie two strings together, you form a knot.
	b. What's a <u>nut</u>?	A nut is a small food that's inside a shell.

B | *PAIRS: Choose a question from Part A. Pronounce the underlined word carefully so your partner can say the correct response.*

---

[1] blunder: *a mistake*

LUCK AND CHANCE

EXERCISE 5: Idioms and Expressions

Natural English

Your English will be more understandable if you group words into meaningful phrases.

I'm surprised that he won.

I'll ask him for the whole week.

A | *Listen to the conversations and complete the sentences with the words you hear. The shaded phrases are idioms or expressions about luck.*

1. **MARAL:** Lee wasn't a good runner. I'm surprised that he won.

   PATRICK: Me, too. But he beat the _____.

2. **MIKA:** Can you come over tonight?

   PETER: No _____ _____. I have to work late.

3. **MARAL:** My boss agreed to give me three days off. I think I'll ask him for the whole week.

   PATRICK: Don't _____ _____ luck. He might take back

   the three days.

B | PAIRS: *Write an idiom from Part A next to the correct definition below.*

Definitions	Idioms
1. try to get too much	_____
2. perform better than expected	_____
3. (something) definitely will not happen	_____

C | PAIRS: *Practice the conversations in Part A. Use the lines to group words together.*

EXERCISE 6: Strange but True

A | *Listen and repeat. Make sure you understand the words.*

rails	injuries	exploded	cliff	mass transportation
haystack	bruises	engine	moral	

B | PAIRS: *Frane (Say "fráhney") Selak was born in Croatia in 1929. Take turns finding out what happened to Selak during his lifetime.*

Student A: Read the information in the chart on page 201 to your partner. Don't show the chart to your partner.

Student B: Take notes to complete the chart on page 205. Don't write every word your partner says. Then read the information already printed in the chart to your partner. Don't show the chart to your partner.

C | CLASS: *Is Selak lucky or unlucky? Explain your answer using events from Selak's life.*

EXERCISE 7: Your Turn

GROUPS: Answer the questions with your classmates.

1. Have you ever won anything?
2. Do you like playing games of chance (the lottery or card games, for example)?
3. Do you consider yourself lucky, unlucky, or neither? Explain.
4. What role do you think luck plays in your life?

STEP 4 EXTENDED PRACTICE

Accuracy Practice *Listen again to Exercises 1 and 2A on page 27. Then record the phrases and words.*

Fluency Practice *Record your answers to the questions in Exercise 7.*

Review: /ɛ/ n**e**t, /æ/ N**a**t, /ə/ n**u**t, and /ɑ/ n**o**t

STEP 1   PRESENTATION

The pictures show how to say /ɛ/, /æ/, /ə/, and /ɑ/.

 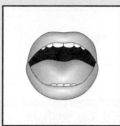 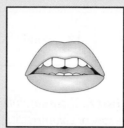 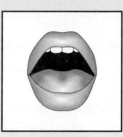

n**e**t /ɛ/	N**a**t /æ/	n**u**t /ə/	n**o**t /ɑ/
Spread your lips a little. Your mouth is almost closed.	Spread your lips. Your mouth is open.	Relax your lips. Your mouth is almost closed.	Relax your lips. Open your mouth.

Spellings for /ɛ/, /æ/, /ə/ and /ɑ/

See Units 4, 5, and 6.

STEP 2   FOCUSED PRACTICE

EXERCISE 1: Words with /ɛ/, /æ/, /ə/, and /ɑ/

A | *Listen and repeat the words. Use the diagrams to help you pronounce the vowels correctly.*

	/ɛ/		/æ/		/ə/		/ɑ/
1.	**a.** net	**b.**	Nat/gnat[1]	**c.**	nut	**d.**	not/knot
2.	**a.** leg	**b.**	lag[2]	**c.**	lug[3]	**d.**	log
3.	**a.** pet	**b.**	pat	**c.**	putt[4]	**d.**	pot
4.	**a.** den	**b.**	Dan	**c.**	done	**d.**	Don

B | *Say a word. Pronounce the vowel carefully. Your classmates will say **a**, **b**, **c**, or **d**.*

---

[1] gnat: *small flying insect;* [2] lag: *to follow behind;* [3] lug: *to carry;* [4] putt: *a short golf shot*

EXERCISE 2: Bingo

A | *Listen to the words on the Bingo card.*

1. lock	**5.** gust	**9.** guest	**13.** c**o**llar
2. c**o**lor	**6.** Don	**10.** K**e**ller	**14.** hum
3. wants	**7.** lack	**11.** ham	**15.** luck
4. hem[1]	**8.** gassed	**12.** done	**16.** once

B | *Now play Bingo. Use the card in Part A. Listen carefully and cross out each word you hear. When you have crossed out a complete row or column [diagram] [diagram] , say "Bingo!"*

EXERCISE 3: Differences in Meaning

A | *Listen to the sentences and responses.*

Sentences	Responses
1. a. Watch out! There's a <u>bog</u> over there!	I've got my boots on.
b. Watch out! There's a <u>bug</u> over there!	I'm not afraid of insects.
2. a. Isn't that a <u>gnat</u> in your soup?	How disgusting! Waiter, take this back!
b. Isn't that a <u>nut</u> in your soup?	Yes, it's made with peanuts.
3. a. What kind of <u>luck</u> do you have?	None—I've never won anything in my life.
b. What kind of <u>lock</u> do you have?	A really strong one—I'm afraid of burglars.
4. a. They made a lot of noise when they <u>left</u>.	Even the neighbors heard the banging doors.
b. They made a lot of noise when they <u>laughed</u>.	The movie was really funny.

B | *PAIRS: Choose a sentence from Part A. Pronounce the underlined word carefully so your partner can say the correct response.*

---

[1] hem: *bottom edge of clothing, turned under to form a clean edge*

EXERCISE 4: Sentences Full of Sounds

A | *Listen to the sentences. Group words into phrases and speak smoothly.*

1. The peppy puppy ate the poppies.
2. Are Dan and Don done in the den?
3. Nat did not put the nuts in the net.
4. The big black bug bled black blood.

B | *PAIRS: Practice the sentences. Take turns.*

STEP 3 COMMUNICATION PRACTICE

HAPPINESS

EXERCISE 5: The Retired CEO and the Fisherman

A | *Listen to the recording and write the words you hear in the blanks. The missing words have /ɛ/, /æ/, /ə/, or /ɑ/ sounds.*

A wealthy, retired[1] CEO[2] was walking on the beach one day when he saw a fisherman. The

fisherman was putting away his nets and other fishing gear.

(continued on next page)

(continued on next page)

---

[1] retired: *stopped working, usually after working many years;* [2] CEO (*an abbreviation for* Chief Executive Officer):
the person with the most power in a large company

RETIRED CEO: How was fishing today? It's pretty early in the day to _____

working, isn't it?

FISHERMAN: The fish weren't biting.[1] So I decided to come in.

RETIRED CEO: Maybe you should try a new _____. You know, you could do a

lot better if you caught more fish.

FISHERMAN: What do you mean? I thought I was doing pretty well.

RETIRED CEO: Well, if you caught more fish, you could buy another boat. You could hire

someone to take the _____ boat out and make even more

money.

FISHERMAN: I _____ that's right.

RETIRED CEO: Yeah, look at me. I worked hard all my life and made a lot of

_____. Now I can take my boat out and go fishing

and come back when I want.

FISHERMAN: But that's _____ what I'm doing now.

Natural English

The word *pretty* can be used as an adverb to increase or decrease the meaning of the next word.

When *pretty* increases meaning, intonation rises on the next word.

It's pretty early to stop working. You should stay a little longer.

When *pretty* decreases meaning, intonation rises on pretty.

Money's pretty important, but not as important as love.

B | *PAIRS: Practice the conversation in Part A. Take turns.*

C | *PAIRS: Answer the questions.*

1. Do the CEO and fisherman have the same definition of success?
2. Do the CEO and fisherman have the same definition of happiness?
3. Do you think the CEO and the fisherman would change places if they could?

---

[1] The fish weren't biting: *The fisherman wasn't catching many fish*

EXERCISE 6: Your Turn

A | *PAIRS: Read the measures of happiness in the left column of the chart. The bold letters are pronounced /ɛ/, /æ/, /ə/, or /ɑ/. Then check (✓) the four measures that are most important to you. Write the reasons for your choices in the right column.*

Measures of Happiness	Why Are These Measures Important to You?
_____ h**a**ving m**o**ney	
_____ owning a home of my own	
_____ h**a**ving a high-paying j**o**b	
_____ h**a**ving a j**o**b that I l**o**ve	
_____ sp**e**nding time with f**a**mily and fr**ie**nds	
_____ h**a**ving a good education	
_____ providing a good education for my children	
_____ driving a nice car	

B | *PAIRS: Compare your choices. Do you and your partner agree?*

STEP 4   EXTENDED PRACTICE

🎧🎤 **Accuracy Practice** *Listen again to Exercises 1A and 4A on pages 31 and 33. Then record the words and sentences.*

🎤 **Fluency Practice** *What are your measures of happiness? Record the measures you checked in Exercise 6A and why they're important to you.*

/r/ after Vowels

The pictures show how to say /r/ after a vowel and the vowel sounds /ər/, /or/, and /ɑr/.

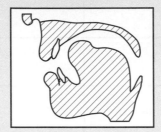

To make /r/ after a vowel, turn the tip of your tongue up and back.

h<u>er</u>, h<u>ur</u>t /ər/   **m<u>ore</u>, f<u>our</u> /or/**   **h<u>ear</u>t, c<u>ar</u> /ɑr/**

Your lips are almost closed.
Keep the inside of your mouth small.
Turn the tip of your tongue up and back.

Round your lips.
Turn the tip of your tongue up and back.

Open your mouth.
Turn the tip of your tongue up and back.

Notes

1. In most dialects of American English, /r/ is pronounced after vowels.

2. *World* is a difficult word to pronounce. Your pronunciation will be clearer if you say *world* as a two-syllable word, stressing the first syllable: /wə́rəld/

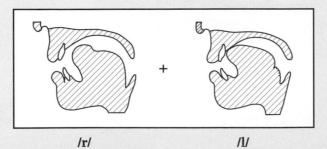

/r/   /l/

Turn the tip of the tongue up and back.

The tip of the tongue touches behind the top teeth.

3. Native speakers shorten some words with *-er* spellings. Listen as your teacher reads the following words.

every: say "évry"   *interest:* say "íntrəst"   *general:* say "génrəl"

several: say "sévrəl"   *temperature:* say "témprətʃər"   *different:* say "díffrənt"

Spellings for /ər/	Spellings for /or/	Spellings for /ɑr/
Common *ir* **bir**d, **cir**cle, **fir**st *ur* **bur**n, **hur**t, **tur**n *er* **her**, s**er**ve, w**er**e	**Common** *or* f**or**, m**or**e, sh**or**t	**Common** *ar* **ar**e, c**ar**, h**ar**d

Other
ear **ear**ly, **ear**th, h**ear**d
wor + consonant
   work, **wor**d,
   worse, **wor**th
	Other
	war **war**, **war**m, **war**n
	oor fl**oor**
		Other
		ear h**ear**t

STEP 2 FOCUSED PRACTICE

EXERCISE 1: Words with /ər/

A | *Listen and repeat the words. Your mouth should be almost closed. Turn the tip of your tongue up and back.*

1. bird	**4.** turn	**7.** her	**10.** worse
2. circle	**5.** hurt	**8.** earth	**11.** word
3. first	**6.** were	**9.** heard	**12.** work

B | *Choose three words and say them to the class.*

EXERCISE 2: Words with /or/ and /ɑr/

A | *Listen and repeat the words. Round your lips for /or/. Open your mouth for /ɑr/. Turn the tip of your tongue up and back for /or/ and /ɑr/.*

/or/		/ɑr/	
1. tore	**4.** formal	**7.** car	**10.** large
2. more	**5.** warm	**8.** start	**11.** heart
3. short	**6.** war	**9.** sharp	**12.** guard

B | *Choose three /or/ words and /ɑr/ words and say them to the class.*

EXERCISE 3: Sounds and Spelling

A | *Listen to the word pairs. Write **S** if the bold sounds are the same. Write **D** if the bold sounds are different.*

1. h**ere**, h**ear** __S__
2. w**ere**, w**ar** _____
3. p**er**fect, p**ar**don _____
4. w**or**k, w**or**d _____
5. b**ur**n, b**ir**d _____
6. w**ar**, w**ore** _____

7. h**er**, h**air** _____
8. h**eard**, h**ard** _____
9. h**ur**t, w**or**d _____
10. w**orse**, w**ore** _____
11. h**eard**, b**eard** _____
12. w**orm**, w**arm** _____

B | *PAIRS: Choose two word pairs that are the same and two word pairs that are different. Say them to your partner.*

EXERCISE 4: Hearing Differences

A | *Listen and write the words you hear in the blanks.*

1. Did you say _____ or _____?
2. Did you say _____ or _____?
3. Did you say _____ or _____?
4. Did you say _____ or _____?
5. Did you say _____ or _____?
6. Did you say _____ or _____?
7. Did you say _____ or _____?

B | *PAIRS: Compare your answers. Then choose a sentence to say to your partner. You can change the order of the words in the blanks. Your partner will tell you which word you said first.*

EXERCISE 5: Listen for Differences: /ər/ vs. /or/ vs. /ɑr/

A | *Listen and repeat the words.*

1.	word	**4.**	war	**7.**	heard	**10.**	heart
2.	hard	**5.**	warn	**8.**	large	**11.**	born
3.	work	**6.**	her	**9.**	pour	**12.**	guard

B | *Write each word in the correct column.*

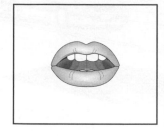  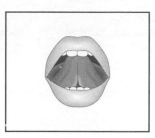

/ər/	/or/	/ɑr/
word		

C | *PAIRS: Compare your lists. Then practice saying the words in each column. Use the diagrams to help you pronounce the words.*

EXERCISE 6: Game: Vowels + *r*

Play this game in two teams—Team A and Team B. Score points for correct answers, correctly pronounced.

Team A: Ask the questions on page 201 to the players on Team B.
Team B: Answer the questions with a word that has the /ər/, /or/, or /ɑr/ sound.
Then ask Team A the questions on page 205.

> **EXAMPLE:**
>
> **TEAM A:** What's three plus one?
>
> **TEAM B:** Four.
>
> **TEAM B:** What's the opposite of *tall*?
>
> **TEAM A:** Short.

WORLD RECORDS

EXERCISE 7: Phrases with *World*

A | *Listen and repeat. Pronounce* **world** *as a two-syllable word: /wərəld/. Make sure you understand the phrases.*

1. a world record
2. the best in the world
3. all over the world
4. set a world record

5. the largest in the whole world
6. break a world record
7. from all corners of the world
8. a world record holder

B | *Listen to the conversation.*

LIN: Here's something I'll bet you don't know. An Irish comedian, Tony Hawks, hitchhiked[1] over 1,600 kilometers (994 miles) with a refrigerator on his back.

ANGELA: What?? How in the world do you know that?

LIN: I got this book of world records for Christmas. It's full of information like that.

ANGELA: Why in the world was he hitchhiking with a refrigerator?

LIN: I think he made a bet with his friend or something like that.

ANGELA: Can I borrow that book? Somebody asked me how many hot dogs you have to eat to hold the world record.

Natural English

Questions that begin *How in the world . . .* , *Why in the world . . .* , and *What in the world . . .* , express the surprise of the speaker. Both the question word and *world* are stressed strongly.

How in the world do you know that?

Why in the world did you eat 20 hot dogs in one hour?

What in the world are you doing out of bed when you're so sick?

C | *PAIRS: Practice the conversation in Part B. Take turns.*

---

[1] hitchhiked: *got a free ride by walking along a road with your arm out and your thumb up*

EXERCISE 8: Your Turn

GROUPS: Answer the questions with your classmates.

1. What world records do you know about?
2. What kinds of people want to set records?
3. Have you ever wanted to set a record for something? Explain.

STEP 4   EXTENDED PRACTICE

Accuracy Practice *Listen again to Exercises 1A and 2A on page 37. Then record the words.*

Fluency Practice *Record your answers to the questions in Exercise 8.*

/ow/ b**oa**t, /ɑ/ p**o**t, and /ɔ/ b**ou**ght

The pictures show how to say /ow/, /ɑ/, and /ɔ/.

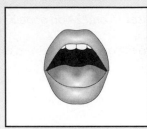

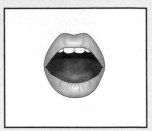

boat, g**o** /ow/	**p**ot, **fa**ther /ɑ/	**b**ought, **cau**ght /ɔ/
Round your lips. /ow/ ends in a /w/ sound.	Open your mouth. Don't round your lips. Pronounce the vowel in the center of your mouth.	Open your mouth and round your lips a little.

Note

When another vowel follows /ow/, use /w/ to join the two vowels.

go^{w}in   show up

Spellings for /ow/	Spellings for /ɑ/	Spellings for /ɔ/

Common
  o go, most, told
  oCe (C is a consonant; *e* is silent) home, rode, those
  oa boat, coat, road
  ow know, show, window
	See Unit 6.	**Common**
		  o + n or *s* long, wrong, lost
		  au caught, audience, August
		  aw awful, draw, law
		  al also, salt, tall

Other
  oe toe, Joe
  ough dough, though
  ew sew
		Other
		  ough ought, thought
		  oa broad

STEP 2 FOCUSED PRACTICE

EXERCISE 1: Words with /ow/, /ɑ/, and /ɔ/

🎧 *Listen and repeat the words.*

/ow/	**/ɑ/**	**/ɔ/**
1. coat	7. rob	13. fought
2. frozen	8. shot	14. thought
3. October	9. cop	15. long
4. show	10. rock	16. loss
5. drove	11. possible	17. caught
6. home	12. modern	18. awful

EXERCISE 2: Dialect Differences: /ɑ/ vs. /ɔ/

Many Americans from the Midwest and West do not use the vowel /ɔ/. They pronounce words like *bought* and *loss* with /ɑ/, the vowel in *pot* and *father*. Many Americans from the Northeast use both the /ɑ/ and /ɔ/ vowels.

🎧 **A** | *Listen to the words. You'll hear each word twice. The first speaker is from Seattle, Washington. This speaker uses the vowel /ɑ/. The second speaker is from New York. The New Yorker uses the vowel /ɔ/. Can you hear the difference in the vowels?*

	Seattle /ɑ/	**New York /ɔ/**
1. fault		
2. bought		
3. loss		
4. thought		
5. taught		
6. long		
7. boss		
8. draw		

🎧 **B** | *Listen again. You'll hear each word once more. Is the speaker from Seattle or New York? If you hear /ɑ/, check (✓) the Seattle column. If you hear /ɔ/, check (✓) the New York column.*

EXERCISE 3: Listen for Differences

A | *Listen and repeat the words.*

1. **a.** wrote	
b. rot	
2. **a.** low	
b. law	
3. **a.** scold	
b. scald	

4. **a.** clothes	
b. claws	
5. **a.** score	
b. scar	
6. **a.** comb[1]	
b. calm[2]	

7. **a.** bold	
b. bald	
8. **a.** coat	
b. cot	
9. **a.** boat	
b. bought	

B | *Listen again and circle the words you hear.*

EXERCISE 4: Differences in Meaning

A | *Listen to the questions and responses.*

Questions	Responses
1. **a.** What do you think of this <u>coat</u>?	It fits you perfectly!
b. What do you think of this <u>cot</u>?	I'd rather have a real bed!
2. **a.** Do you think he was <u>cold</u>?	Yes. His lips were blue, and his teeth were chattering.
b. Do you think he was <u>called</u>?	Yes. Nancy said she spoke to him last night.
3. **a.** What happened? That's a horrible <u>scar</u>!	I cut myself.
b. What happened? That's a horrible <u>score</u>!	I didn't study.
4. **a.** How do you spell *law*?	L-A-W.
b. How do you spell *low*?	L-O-W.

Natural English

Be sure to clearly pronounce the vowels in the words *law* and *low*. You can pronounce *law* with the vowel /ɑ/ (the same vowel in *father*). Pronounce *low* with the vowel /ow/.

   a low-cost law firm

B | *PAIRS: Choose a question from Part A. Pronounce the underlined word carefully so your partner can say the correct response.*

---

[1] *In* comb, *the* b *is silent;* [2] *In* calm, *the* l *is silent.*

HOME

EXERCISE 5: What Does *Home* Mean?

🎧 **A** | *Listen to the three views of home and take notes.*

Sanctuary[1]	Gathering Place	Pit Stop[2]

B | *GROUPS: Explain the three speakers' views of their homes.*

---

[1] sanctuary: *a safe place;* [2] pit stop: *a very quick stop that race-car drivers make to change tires, get gas, etc.*

EXERCISE 6: Your Turn

A | *Read the questions and write your answers in the chart.*

Questions	Your Name _____	Your Partner's Name _____	Your Partner's Name _____
Where are you living now? (house, apartment, dorm room, etc.)			
Do you think "home" should be a sanctuary, a gathering place, or a pit stop?			
Who do you live with?			
How do you feel if people visit without calling first?			
When you have free time, would you rather stay home or go out?			
Do you like to entertain¹ at home?			
What was your home like when you were a child?			

B | *GROUPS: Work in groups of three. Ask your partners the questions in the chart and write their answers in the correct columns.*

STEP 4 EXTENDED PRACTICE

Accuracy Practice *Listen again to Exercises 1 and 3A on pages 43 and 44. Then record the words.*

Fluency Practice *Make a short recording describing your present home.*

---

¹ to entertain: *to treat someone as a guest by giving them food and drink*

STEP 1 PRESENTATION

The pictures show how to say /uw/ and /ʊ/.

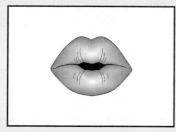

f<u>oo</u>d, d<u>o</u> /uw/

Round your lips tightly.
/uw/ ends in a /w/ sound.

b<u>oo</u>k, c<u>ou</u>ld /ʊ/

Your lips are less rounded
for /ʊ/ than for /uw/.

Note

When another vowel follows /uw/, join the two vowels with /w/.

Do^wit.   Who^wis it?

Spellings for /uw/	Spellings for /ʊ/
Common *oo* c**oo**l, n**oo**n, ch**oo**se *u* st**u**dent, tr**u**th, revol**u**tion	**Common** *oo* f**oo**t, g**oo**d, h**oo**d *u* p**u**t, p**u**sh, s**u**gar
Other *o* d**o**, wh**o**, m**o**ve *ou* gr**ou**p, thr**ou**gh *ew* n**ew**, gr**ew** *ui* s**ui**t, j**ui**ce *eau* b**eau**ty	**Other** *ou(ld)* w**ou**ld, c**ou**ld, sh**ou**ld *o* w**o**man

STEP 2 FOCUSED PRACTICE

EXERCISE 1: Words with /uw/ and /ʊ/

🎧 *Listen and repeat the words.*

	/uw/				/ʊ/		
1.	threw	**5.**	blue	**9.**	book	**13.**	could
2.	include	**6.**	soon	**10.**	look	**14.**	should
3.	introduce	**7.**	truth	**11.**	woman	**15.**	sugar
4.	fool	**8.**	move	**12.**	put	**16.**	hood

EXERCISE 2: Listen for Differences: /uw/ vs. /ʊ/

🎧 **A |** *Listen and repeat the words.*

1.	**a.** Luke	**3.**	**a.** cooed²	**5.**	**a.** who'd	**7.**	**a.** stewed⁴
	b. look		**b.** could		**b.** hood		**b.** stood
2.	**a.** suit	**4.**	**a.** shooed³	**6.**	**a.** pool	**8.**	**a.** fool
	b. soot¹		**b.** should		**b.** pull		**b.** full

🎧 **B |** *Listen again and circle the words you hear.*

EXERCISE 3: Rhyme

🎧 **A |** *Listen to the rhyme.*

How much wood would a woodchuck⁵ chuck⁶

If a woodchuck could chuck wood?

Just as much as a woodchuck would

If a woodchuck could chuck wood.

B | *PAIRS: Practice the rhyme. Group words together.*

---

¹ soot: *black ash;* ² coo: *to make a low soft sound;* ³ shoo: *to wave someone away;* ⁴ stewed: *slowly cooked meats and vegetables;* ⁵ woodchuck: *a small animal that has thick brown fur and lives in holes in the ground;*
⁶ chuck (slang): *to throw*

48 UNIT 10

EXERCISE 4: Phrases and Idioms with /uw/ and /ʊ/

A | *Listen to the idioms in the left column. The bold letters are pronounced /uw/ or /ʊ/.*

Idioms		Definitions
_c_ **1.** black and bl**ue**	**a.**	please yourself
____ **2.** p**u**ll something off	**b.**	an opportunity to enter something
____ **3.** s**ui**t yourself	¢.	bruised[1]
____ **4.** tr**ue** to form	**d.**	fight ferociously
____ **5.** p**u**t up with	**e.**	endure, tolerate
____ **6.** f**oo**d for thought	**f.**	following a pattern
____ **7.** (have) a f**oo**t in the door	**g.**	something to think about
____ **8.** fight t**oo**th and nail	**h.**	do something even if it's difficult

B | *PAIRS: Match each idiom with its definition. Then check your answers with the class.*

EXERCISE 5: Conversations

A | *PAIRS: Complete the sentences with idioms from Exercise 4A.*

1. JOE: Was June hurt in the accident?

MARCELLA: She was _____ _____ _____ all over,

but she didn't have any broken bones.

2. MARCELLA: Your roommate is so messy! How do you stand it?

JOE: He lets me use his car, and I _____ _____

_____ his mess.

3. JOE: Do you really think I can get that job on the "News Hour"?

MARCELLA: Well, I'd say you already have _____ _____

_____ _____ _____—you're dating

the producer's daughter!

(continued on next page)

———————

[1] bruised: *dark mark on the skin caused by an injury*

4. MARCELLA: I know you don't approve, but I'm going to buy that sports car!

JOE: OK, but here's some _____ _____

_____: Don't forget that you have to pay for the gas!

B | *PAIRS: Practice the conversations in Part A. Take turns.*

STEP 3 COMMUNICATION PRACTICE

DILEMMAS

EXERCISE 6: Favoritism on the Job

Favoritism at work involves treating some employees better than others because of personal characteristics or connections rather than work performance.

A | *Listen and repeat. Make sure you understand the words.*

lifeguard	sports center	(work) shift	hourly wage

B | *Listen to the recording and then answer the questions.*

1. How did Jane get her summer job?
2. Why was Jane happy about her work shifts?
3. How does Jane feel about other employees at the gym?
4. Describe the lifeguard.
5. Why does Jane feel guilty?
6. What should Jane do?

C | *GROUPS: Discuss your answers to the questions.*

EXERCISE 7: Dilemmas: *Could, should,* and *would*

A | *A "dilemma" is a problem that doesn't have an easy solution. Read Max's dilemmas. Then write three solutions. Use* **could** *to describe possible things Max could do. Use* **should** *to give Max advice. Use* **'d (would)** *to say what you would do in the same situation.*

1. While Max is parking his car, he hits the car behind him and breaks its headlight. No one else sees the accident.

   What could Max do? _____

   What should Max do? _____

   What would you do in this situation? _____

2. Max's classmate, June, asks Max if she can copy his homework.

   What could Max do? _____

   What should Max do? _____

   What would you do in this situation? _____

3. The cashier in the restaurant gives Max an extra ten dollars in change.

   What could Max do? _____

   What should Max do? _____

   What would you do in this situation? _____

Natural English

The letter *l* in *could, should,* and *would* is not pronounced.

What cou/d he do?

What shou/d he do?

What wou/d you do?

B | *GROUPS: Discuss your solutions to Max's dilemmas in Part A.*

STEP 4 EXTENDED PRACTICE

Accuracy Practice *Listen again to Exercises 1 and 2A on page 48. Then record the words.*

Fluency Practice *Record a dilemma that you're facing. Describe some possible solutions using* **could** *and/or* **should**.

CONSONANTS

UNIT	PRONUNCIATION FOCUS	COMMUNICATION PRACTICE
11	Consonant Overview	Smart Animals
12	Beginning and Final Consonants	Cutting Back
13	Past Tense Endings	The Would-Be Thief
14	*TH* Sounds: /θ/ thanks and /ð/ that	Birthdays
15	/p/ pie, /b/ buy, /f/ fine, /v/ vine, and /w/ wine	Fears and Phobias
16	/s/ seven and /z/ zero	Life Lessons and Others' Advice
17	/ʃ/ shoe and /ʒ/ television	Time Off
18	/tʃ/ chicken and /dʒ/ jacket	Changing Jobs
19	-*S* Endings: Plurals, Possessives, and Present Tense	Time Management
20	/r/ right and /l/ light	Going Places
21	/m/ mouse, /n/ nose, and /ŋ/ sing	Free Time
22	/y/ yet and /dʒ/ jet; Consonant Clusters with /y/: regular	Connected
23	/h/ hat; Reduction of *H* Words	Weather
24	Beginning Consonant Clusters	Breaking Up
25	Final Consonant Clusters; Joining Words Together	I Need a Rest

UNIT 11 Consonant Overview

STEP 1 PRESENTATION

There are 24 consonants in English. Listen to the words.

pie /p/	pre**ss**ure /ʃ/
buy /b/	plea**s**ure /ʒ/
tie /t/	**ch**ain /tʃ/
die /d/	**J**ane /dʒ/
came /k/	**r**ight /r/
game /g/	**l**ight /l/
fairy /f/	so**m**e /m/
very /v/	su**n** /n/
thin /θ/	su**ng** /ŋ/
then /ð/	**y**es /y/
Sue /s/	**w**et /w/
zoo /z/	**h**ead /h/

Notes

The pronunciation of final consonants depends on the sound that begins the next word:

1. Final Consonant + Vowel: *stand up*

   Final consonants join clearly to words that begin with vowels.

2. Final Consonant + Same Consonant: *half full*

   When a word ends in a consonant and the next word begins with the same consonant, say one long consonant (written "⌒"). Don't say the consonant twice.

3. Final Consonant + Different Consonant: *black bag*

   When a word ends in a consonant and the next word begins with a different consonant, keep the final consonant short (written " ᵎ "). Don't separate the two words: Say the next word immediately after the final consonant.

EXERCISE 1: Consonants Made with the Lips

PAIRS: Look at your partner and say **B** *slowly. How do your lips look? What other consonants are made with the lips? Write the consonants and a sample word for each one below.*

	Consonants	Words
1.	_____	_____
2.	_____	_____
3.	_____	_____
4.	_____	_____
5.	_____	_____

EXERCISE 2: Other Consonants

A | *Look at the mouth diagrams.*

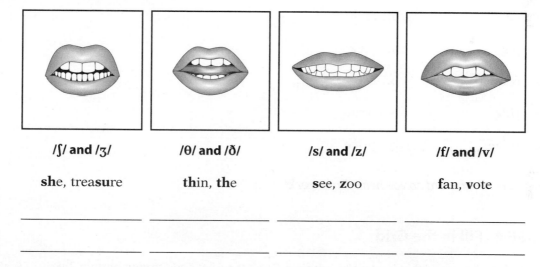

/ʃ/ and /ʒ/	/θ/ and /ð/	/s/ and /z/	/f/ and /v/
she, trea**s**ure	**th**in, **th**e	**s**ee, **z**oo	**f**an, **v**ote

_____ _____ _____ _____

_____ _____ _____ _____

B | *PAIRS: Face your partner and say the words in the box below slowly. Exaggerate the bold sound in each word. Your partner will look at your lips as you say the bold sound and write the word under the matching diagram in Part A. Take turns.*

ki**ss**	wi**th**	lau**gh**	wa**sh**	bee**s**	bo**th**	**f**ive	mea**s**ure

EXERCISE 3: Voiced and Voiceless Consonants

A | *Consonants are voiced or voiceless. The vocal cords vibrate when you make a voiced sound like /z/. They don't vibrate when you make a voiceless sound like /s/. You can feel the vibration with your hand.*

1. Put your fingers against the side of your throat.
2. Make a long /zzzzzz/, and feel the vibration.
3. Make a long /ssssss/. What do you feel?
4. Switch back and forth between the two sounds: /zzzzzz-ssssss-zzzzzz-ssssss/
5. Repeat steps 1–3, using /vvvvvvv/ and /fffffff/. Is /v/ voiced or voiceless? Is /f/ voiced or voiceless?

B | *Vowels before voiced consonants are usually longer than vowels before voiceless consonants. Listen and repeat the words. Make the vowels before voiced consonants long.*

	Voiced		**Voiceless**
1.	a. lea**ve**	b.	lea**f**
2.	a. pea**s**	b.	pea**ce**
3.	a. ri**se**	b.	ri**ce**
4.	a. e**dge**	b.	e**tch**[1]
5.	a. pi**g**	b.	pi**ck**
6.	a. ro**be**	b.	ro**pe**
7.	a. ri**de**	b.	wri**te**
8.	a. pri**ze**	b.	pri**ce**

C | *Listen again. Which word do you hear? Circle **a** or **b**.*

EXERCISE 4: Fill in the Grid

PAIRS: Each of you has a grid that is partially complete. Don't show your grid to your partner. Take turns asking each other for missing words. When you finish, compare your grids. They should be the same. Students A's grid is on page 202. Student B's grid is on page 205.

What's in box A2?

---

[1] etch: *to cut designs into metal or glass*

56 UNIT 11

EXERCISE 5: Conversation

A | *Listen to the conversation. Circle the word* **that**.

IRENA:　I've been trying to teach my cat to roll over.

WILLIAM:　You can't teach a cat to do tricks. They're too independent. Why do you want to teach it to roll over?

IRENA:　My neighbor has a parrot that talks. She says her parrot is smarter than my cat.

WILLIAM:　Parrots don't really talk. They just imitate human sounds, but that's not talking.

Natural English

The word *that* is unstressed and short when it's a conjunction. The conjunction is usually grouped with the following clause.

My neighbor has a parrot that talks.

When *that* is a demonstrative pronoun or adjective, it's stressed.

Thát's not talking.

B | *PAIRS: Practice the conversation in Part A. Take turns.*

STEP 3　COMMUNICATION PRACTICE

SMART ANIMALS

EXERCISE 6: Ruby the Octopus

A | *Listen and repeat the words and phrases. Notice how final consonants in phrases join to following words.*

1. octopus
2. take the lid off a jar
3. aquarium
4. shrimp
5. figure out
6. adapts easily

B | *Listen to the recording. Then read the statements below. Write* **T (True)** *or* **F (False)** *next to each statement. Correct the false statements.*

_____ **1.** Ruby was a bear.

_____ **2.** Ruby lived in an aquarium.

_____ **3.** Ruby learned how to open a box.

_____ **4.** Hall believes that Ruby has strong problem-solving skills.

C | *GROUPS: Do you think what Ruby learned to do shows intelligence? Why or why not? Discuss.*

EXERCISE 7: Comparing Intelligence

A | *Read the animal names in the chart. Then rank the animals from the most intelligent* **(1)** *to least intelligent* **(8).**

Animals	Intelligence	What can these animals learn to do?
Dolphin		
Horse		
Chimpanzee		
Dog		
Cat		
Parrot		
Crow		
Salmon		

B | *GROUPS: Compare your charts. Then answer the questions.*

1. Have you ever had a pet? If so, what kind?
2. Did you ever try to teach it something? Explain.

STEP 4 EXTENDED PRACTICE

Accuracy Practice *Listen again to Exercise 3B on page 56. Then record the words.*

Fluency Practice *Record your answers to the questions in Exercise 7B.*

Beginning and Final Consonants

Beginning Voiceless Stop Consonants: /p/, /t/, /k/

1. Pronounce /p/, /t/, and /k/ with aspiration (a strong puff of air) when they begin a one-syllable word (').

    pʰan   tʰoo   cʰome

2. Pronounce /p/, /t/, and /k/ with aspiration when they begin a stressed syllable.

    repʰéat   retʰúrn   acʰádemy

Joining Final Consonants to the Next Word

1. **Final Consonant + Vowel:** *fresh air*

    Join the consonant and vowel clearly.

2. **Final Consonant + Same Consonant:** *half full*

    Say one long consonant. Don't say the consonant twice.

3. **Final Consonant + Different Consonant:** *good people*

    Say the final consonant, but keep it short. Say the next word immediately. Don't pronounce the final consonant strongly. Don't separate the two consonants with a vowel sound.

Vowels Before Final Voiced and Voiceless Consonants: *made, make*

Vowels before voiced consonants are longer than vowels before voiceless consonants.

    Longer vowels: made   laid   prove   rise
    Shorter vowels: make   late   proof   rice

EXERCISE 1: Aspiration

A | *Listen and repeat the words. Aspirate the beginning consonant: Pronounce it strongly with a puff of air.*

1. pˡay
2. pˡublic
3. depˡend
4. appˡly
5. tˡell
6. tˡake
7. attˡend
8. retˡire
9. kˡey
10. cˡut
11. occˡur
12. accˡount

B | *The consonants /p/, /t/, and /k/ are aspirated only before stressed vowels. Listen to the words. Place a stress mark (ˈ) over the stressed vowel in each word. Write **A** in the blank if the bold consonant is aspirated. Write **U** if it is not aspirated.*

1. ópen __U__
2. appear _____
3. today _____
4. attack _____
5. accomplish _____
6. bacon _____

C | *PAIRS: Compare your answers with a partner. Then practice saying the words. Take turns.*

EXERCISE 2: Listen for Differences

A | *Listen and repeat the words. The vowels in the a words precede voiced consonants. The vowels in the b words precede voiceless consonants. Make the vowels in the a words longer than the vowels in the b words.*

1. a. had
   b. hat
2. a. cab
   b. cap
3. a. robe
   b. rope
4. a. seed
   b. seat
5. a. stayed
   b. state
6. a. said
   b. set
7. a. dug
   b. duck
8. a. pig
   b. pick
9. a. log
   b. lock

B | *Listen again and circle the words you hear.*

EXERCISE 3: Joining Final Consonants

A | *Listen to the phrases.*

Final Consonant + Vowel	**Final Consonant + Same Consonant**
1. a. Miss Anderson	**b.** Miss Sanderson
2. a. keep ants	**b.** keep pants
3. a. wrote "L"	**b.** wrote "tell"
4. a. take oats[1]	**b.** take coats
5. a. kiss Andy	**b.** kiss Sandy
6. a. love Ann	**b.** love Van
7. a. hug[2] us	**b.** hug Gus
8. a. chase Ally	**b.** chase Sally

B | *Listen again and circle the phrases you hear.*

C | *PAIRS: Say a phrase from Part A. Your partner will tell you which phrase you said.*

EXERCISE 4: Listen for Final Consonants

Listen and complete the sentences with phrases from Exercise 3.

1. Did you invite _____ or _____?

2. _____ _____ inside; _____ _____ outside.

3. You _____ _____, and I _____ _____.

4. You _____ _____ to the cleaners; you _____ _____ to the horses.

5. You _____ _____, and I'll _____ _____.

6. I _____ _____, and you _____ _____.

7. If you _____ _____, you should also _____ _____.

8. You _____ _____, and I'll _____ _____.

---

[1] *oats:* a grain or cereal; [2] *hug:* to put your arms around someone in love or friendship

CUTTING BACK

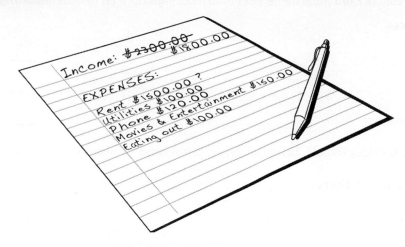

EXERCISE 5: Cutting Expenses

A | *Listen to the conversation and complete the sentences with the words you hear.*

DAVID: What's the matter, Kasha?

KASHA: My boss told me he's going to _____ _____ my hours. He says he doesn't want to, but he has to.

DAVID: _____ _____ going to mean for you?

KASHA: I'm not sure. I don't know how many hours I'll lose. But I don't know if I'll be able to keep _____ _____.

DAVID: Maybe you could get a _____. You have the space.

KASHA: I know. But I really don't _____ _____.

Natural English

When you shorten an infinitive, your voice goes up on the verb and down on *to*.

She doesn't want to, but she has to.

B | *PAIRS: Practice the conversation. Take turns.*

EXERCISE 6: Your Turn

GROUPS: Like people during tough economic times, governments may also have to cut back on expenses and the services they provide. Read the list of services below. Which ones do you think the government should cut back on? Rank the services from most important (1) to least important (6).

Government Services

1. education   _____

2. health care   _____

3. retirement/pensions[1]   _____

4. transportation services (roads, bridges, trains, buses, and subways)   _____

5. security (police and military)   _____

6. farming assistance   _____

STEP 4 EXTENDED PRACTICE

Accuracy Practice *Listen again to Exercise 3A on page 62. Then record the phrases.*

Fluency Practice *If you needed to spend less money, what would you cut back on? Record your answer to the question.*

---

[1] pension: *the money that a company pays regularly to someone after retirement*

UNIT 13 Past Tense Endings

STEP 1 PRESENTATION

The regular past tense *-ed* ending can be pronounced as a syllable or a sound.

1. Pronounce the *-ed* ending as a new syllable (/əd/ or /ɪd/) when the base verb ends in /t/ or /d/.

    lan<u>d</u> — It landed at 8:00 P.M.

2. Pronounce the *-ed* ending as /t/ or /d/ when the base verb ends in other sounds.
    a. Use /t/ when the base verb ends in a voiceless sound (/p, k, θ, f, s, ʃ, tʃ/).

    ki<u>ss</u> — He "kisst" (kissed) his mother.

    b. Use /d/ when the base verb ends in a vowel or voiced sound (/b, g, ð, v, z, ʒ, dʒ, m, n, ŋ, r, l/).

    op<u>en</u> — I "opend" (opened) the door.

STEP 2 FOCUSED PRACTICE

EXERCISE 1: Listen for Syllables

A | *Listen and repeat the present and past tense verbs.*

1. **a.** repeat __2__
    b. repeated __3__

2. **a.** decide _____
    b. decided _____

3. **a.** investigate _____
    b. investigated _____

4. **a.** end _____
    b. ended _____

5. **a.** create _____
    b. created _____

6. **a.** paint _____
    b. painted _____

7. **a.** expect _____
    b. expected _____

8. **a.** add _____
    b. added _____

9. **a.** arrest _____
    b. arrested _____

B | *Underline the syllables in each verb. Then write the number of syllables in the blanks.*

C | *Review the rules in Step 1 on page 65. Then complete the sentences.*

1. All of the present tense verbs in Part A end in a _____ sound or a

   _____ sound.

2. The past tense endings of these verbs are pronounced as a new _____.

EXERCISE 2: Hearing Endings

A | *Listen and repeat the word pairs.*

1. **a.** stop

   b. stopped _____

2. **a.** call

   b. called _____

3. **a.** reach

   b. reached _____

4. **a.** hug

   b. hugged _____

5. **a.** ask

   b. asked _____

6. **a.** believe

   b. believed _____

7. **a.** dream

   b. dreamed _____

8. **a.** continue

   b. continued _____

B | *How is the past tense ending pronounced? Write /t/ or /d/ in the blanks.*

EXERCISE 3: Apply the Rule

A | *PAIRS: How is the past tense ending of each verb below pronounced? If the -ed ending is a new syllable, write* **syllable** *in the blank. If the -ed ending is a final sound (/t/ or /d/), write* **sound**.

1. want _____*syllable*_____

2. enjoy _____

3. vote _____

4. wash _____

5. demand _____

6. help _____

7. study _____

8. clean _____

B | *Say both the past and present tense of each verb. Take turns.*

C | *Review the rules in Step 1 on page 65. Then circle the correct answer to complete the sentence.*

The past tense endings of the verbs in Part A (are/are not) pronounced as an extra syllable.

EXERCISE 4: Past Tense Game

Play this game in two teams—Team A and Team B. Give points for correct answers, pronounced correctly.

Team A: Read the verbs on page 202 to the players on Team B.
Team B: Answer with the past tense of the verbs. Then read the verbs on page 205 to Team A. Follow the example.

> **EXAMPLE:**
>
> **TEAM A:** call
>
> **TEAM B:** called

EXERCISE 5: Conversations

A | *Listen and repeat the phrases. Join final consonants and beginning vowels.*

looked at three	seemed angry	waited all day
ordered it	started over	watched awhile

B | *PAIRS: Complete the sentences with phrases from the box. Then practice the conversations. Take turns.*

1. **A:** Did you see the game?

   B: I _____, but then I fell asleep.

2. **A:** Did you find a new apartment?

   B: No. I _____ apartments, but they were all too small.

3. **A:** Are you still working on that essay?

   B: Yes. I didn't like what I'd written, so I _____.

4. **A:** Did you find the book you need?

   B: Not at the bookstore, but I _____ online.

5. **A:** Did the cable repairman come?

   B: No. I _____, but he never showed up.

6. **A:** How are you?

   B: I'm fine. How are you? You _____ this morning.

EXERCISE 6: Present Tense vs. Past Tense

A | *Listen to the conversations. Circle the verbs you hear. Then write* **do** *or* **did** *in the blanks.*

1. **IVAN:**   I (need/(needed)) some money.

   SYLVIA: So _____*did*_____ I.

2. **IVAN:**   I (travel/traveled) a lot.

   SYLVIA: So _____ I.

3. **IVAN:**   I (work/worked) so hard.

   SYLVIA: So _____ I.

4. **IVAN:**   I (help/helped) Mom and Dad a lot.

   SYLVIA: So _____ I.

5. **IVAN:**   I (clean/cleaned) on Saturday.

   SYLVIA: So _____ I.

B | *PAIRS: Practice the conversations. When you say Ivan's part, choose the present or the past tense. Your partner will decide how to answer, using* **do** *or* **did**. *Take turns.*

EXERCISE 7: The Weekend

A | *Use the lines below to write positive sentences about what you did last weekend. Use past tense verbs.*

_____

_____

_____

_____

B | *PAIRS: Take turns reading your sentences. If you did the same thing as your partner, say "So did I."*

THE WOULD-BE THIEF

EXERCISE 8: The Convenience Store

Natural English

Use *would-be* as an adjective to describe people who are unsuccessful or frustrated in satisfying their ambitions.

The word *would* receives more stress than *be*. Listen as your teacher reads the examples.

the wóuld-be thíef

a wóuld-be áctor

A | *Listen and repeat. Make sure you understand the words.*

1. thief

2. convenience store

3. rob

4. battery-powered saw

5. collapse

6. judge

B | *Listen to the story twice. As you listen the second time, write the past tense verbs you hear.*

_____

_____

_____

EXERCISE 9: Scrambled Sentences

A | *PAIRS: Put the sentences in order so they tell the story of "The Would-Be Thief." Then circle the pronunciation of the past tense endings.*

Sentences	Past Tense Endings
_____ He dropped onto the roof.	/əd/ /t/ /d/
_____ The roof collapsed.	/əd/ /t/ /d/
_____ He climbed the tree.	/əd/ /t/ /d/
_____ He drove to the convenience store.	Irregular verb
_____ He crashed onto the table.	/əd/ /t/ /d/
_____ He entered the parking lot behind the store.	/əd/ /t/ /d/
_____ The police arrested him.	/əd/ /t/ /d/
_____ He turned off his car lights.	/əd/ /t/ /d/
_1_ He decided to rob the convenience store.	(/əd/) /t/ /d/
_____ He started to saw a hole in the roof.	/əd/ /t/ /d/

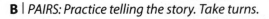

B | *PAIRS: Practice telling the story. Take turns.*

C | *PAIRS: Answer the questions.*
   1. Why is the thief only a *would-be* thief? What did he do wrong?
   2. What do you think happened to the thief?

STEP 4 EXTENDED PRACTICE

🎧 🎤 **Accuracy Practice** *Listen again to Exercise 2A on page 66. Then record the word pairs.*

🎤 **Fluency Practice** *Record a different ending for "The Would-Be Thief." Use past tense verbs in your story.*

TH Sounds: /θ/ <u>th</u>anks and /ð/ <u>th</u>at

STEP 1 PRESENTATION

Look at the pictures. They show how to say /θ/ and /ð/.

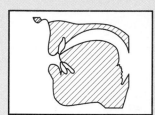 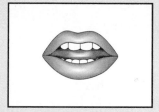

<u>th</u>anks, <u>th</u>ree /θ/
<u>th</u>at, <u>th</u>ose /ð/

The tip of your tongue is between your teeth.

/θ/ is voiceless.
/ð/ is voiced.

Notes

1. You have to pronounce the *-th* in *cloth*, but not in *clothes*.

   Clothes is pronounced like the verb (to) *close*.

2. Final /θ/ or /ð/ may be simplified or deleted when an *-s* ending is added.

   one mon<u>th</u> /nθ/ — two mon<u>ths</u> /nts/

   one-fif<u>th</u> /fθ/ — two-fif<u>ths</u> /fs/

Spellings for /θ/	Spellings for /ð/
th <u>th</u>ing, heal<u>th</u>y, bo<u>th</u>	*th* <u>th</u>is, o<u>th</u>er, wea<u>th</u>er *the* (final) brea<u>the</u>, ba<u>the</u>
Exceptions: Pronounce the *th* of *Thai*, *Thailand*, and *Thames* as /t/.	

EXERCISE 1: Words with /θ/

Listen and repeat the words.

1. thing	**5.** nothing	**9.** tooth
2. think	**6.** something	**10.** mouth
3. thanks	**7.** healthy	**11.** fifth
4. thousand	**8.** birthday	**12.** death

EXERCISE 2: Words with /ð/

Listen and repeat the words.

1. this	**5.** weather	**9.** rather
2. that	**6.** together	**10.** smooth
3. those	**7.** other	**11.** bathe
4. there	**8.** mother	**12.** breathe

EXERCISE 3: Listen for Differences

A | *Listen and repeat the words.*

1. **a.** thing	**3.** **a.** three	**5.** **a.** then
b. sing	**b.** tree	**b.** Zen
2. **a.** with	**4.** **a.** breathe	**6.** **a.** thanks
b. wit	**b.** breeze	**b.** tanks

B | *Say a word from Part A. Your partner will tell you which word you said.*

EXERCISE 4: Game: *TH* sounds

Play this game in two teams—Team A and Team B. Give points for correct answers, correctly pronounced.

Team A: Ask the questions on page 202 to the players on Team B.
Team B: Answer the questions with a word or phrase that has the *TH* sound. Then ask Team A the questions on page 206.

> **EXAMPLE:**
>
> **Team A:** What's thirty plus three (30 + 3)?
> **Team B:** Thirty-three.

EXERCISE 5: Sentences Full of Sounds

A | *Listen to the sentences.*

1. The fourth Thursday of November is Thanksgiving.
2. A "thingamajig" is something whose real name you can't think of.
3. Three hundred thirty-three thousand therapists thought about the new theory of thinking.
4. The thieves threatened three dozen southern mothers.*
5. Wetter weather and thunderstorms are expected this month in northern states.

B | *PAIRS: Practice saying the sentences. Group words into phrases and speak smoothly.*

> ***Natural English**
>
> In the direction words *south* and *north*, *th* is pronounced /θ/.
>
> In the adjectives *southern* and *northern*, *th* is pronounced /ð/. Also, in *southern*, the first vowel is pronounced /ə/, not /ɑw/.
>
> /səðərn/ (southern) mothers
>
> /norðərn/ (northern) fathers

STEP 3 COMMUNICATION PRACTICE

BIRTHDAYS

EXERCISE 6: When's Your Birthday?

Ask your classmates when their birthdays are. Write each student's name and birth date in the chart. Do any of your classmates have the same birthday (month and day)?

January	February	March	April	May	June
July	August	September	October	November	December

EXERCISE 7: Milestone Birthdays

🎧 **A** | *Listen and repeat. Make sure you understand the words.*

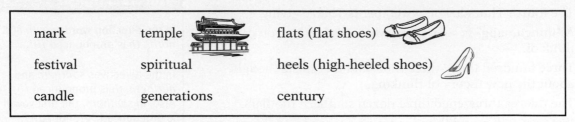

mark	temple	flats (flat shoes)
festival	spiritual	heels (high-heeled shoes)
candle	generations	century

🎧 **B** | *Listen to the recording and then answer the questions.*

1. What's the name of the festival that's celebrated on November 15th of each year in Japan?
2. Why is the thirteenth birthday important to people living in English-speaking countries?
3. How do people in Latin American countries celebrate a girl's fifteenth birthday?
4. The eighteenth birthday is important in America. Why?

C | *GROUPS: Compare your answers to the questions. Then tell your classmates about important milestone birthdays in your country.*

STEP 4 EXTENDED PRACTICE

🎧🎤 **Accuracy Practice** *Listen again to Exercises 1 and 2 on page 72. Then record the words.*

🎤 **Fluency Practice** *Choose two birthdays that are special in your country. Record an explanation of why they're special.*

UNIT 15 /p/ pie, /b/ buy, /f/ fine, /v/ vine, and /w/ wine

STEP 1 PRESENTATION

The pictures show how to say /p/, /b/, /f/, /v/, and /w/.

 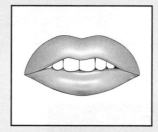 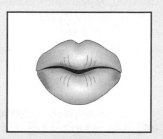

pie /p/	fine /f/	wine /w/
buy /b/	vine /v/	

Close your lips.

/p/ is voiceless.
/b/ is voiced.

Touch your top teeth
against the inside of
your lower lip.
Your lower lip protrudes
(sticks out) a little.

/f/ is voiceless.
/v/ is voiced.

Start with your lips
rounded. Then
unround them.

Notes

1. If your native language is Korean, you may pronounce *question* like "kestion" instead of "kwestion." If this is a problem, round your lips to make the /w/ sound.

2. If your native language is Japanese or Korean, you may pronounce *woman* and *would* like "'oman" and "'ood." If this is a problem, try these tips:

   a. Say, "Way-would, way-would, way-would." When you say *would*, your lips should move the way they move when you say *way*.

   b. Start with your lips rounded and then unround them as you say *woman*. Unrounding creates the /w/ sound at the beginning of a word.

   c. Make two /u/ sounds. Stress the second /u/: uúman (woman).

   d. Stretch a rubber band as you say the beginning of *woman* and *would*.

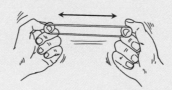

(continued on next page)

Spellings for /p/, /b/, /f/, /v/, and /w/	
Common /p/, /b/, /f/, /v/, and /w/ are usually spelled with the letters *p*, *b*, *f*, *v*, and *w*.	**Silent Letters** *Silent* p: p̸sychology, receip̸t, rasp̸berry *Silent* b: thumb̸, comb̸, climb̸ *Silent* w: w̸rite, w̸reath, answ̸er
Other /f/ 　*ph* al**ph**abet, tele**ph**one 　*gh* enou**gh**, lau**gh**, tou**gh** /w/ 　*u* q**u**estion, sq**u**are, lang**u**age 　*wh* **wh**en, **wh**ere, **wh**ite 　unwritten /w/: once, one	

STEP 2   FOCUSED PRACTICE

EXERCISE 1: Words with /p/ and /b/

Listen and repeat the words.

	/p/				/b/		
1.	person	5.	cup	9.	best	13.	rob
2.	pink	6.	stop	10.	begin	14.	somebody
3.	copy	7.	people	11.	lobby	15.	Bobby
4.	happy	8.	population	12.	about	16.	baby

EXERCISE 2: Words with /f/ and /v/

Listen and repeat the words.

	/f/				/v/		
1.	fear	5.	laugh	9.	very	13.	give
2.	finish	6.	belief	10.	voice	14.	have
3.	awful	7.	fulfill	11.	never	15.	vivid
4.	difficult	8.	falafel[1]	12.	heaven	16.	olive

---

[1] falafel: *a Middle Eastern food made from fried chickpeas and spices*

EXERCISE 3: Words with /w/

🎧 *Listen and repeat the words.*

1. woman
2. would
3. walk
4. away
5. language
6. quietly
7. quick
8. twenty
9. question

EXERCISE 4: Listen for Differences

🎧 **A** | *Listen and repeat the words.*

1. **a.** berry
   b. very
   c. wary[1]

2. **a.** pine
   b. fine
   c. wine

3. **a.** bull
   b. full
   c. wool

4. **a.** pest[2]
   b. vest
   c. west

5. **a.** pear
   b. fair
   c. wear

6. **a.** Pow!
   b. vow
   c. Wow!

🎧 **B** | *Listen again and circle the words you hear.*

EXERCISE 5: Mouth Shapes

A | *PAIRS: Choose one word from each set in Exercise 4A. Face your partner and say the word without using any sound ("mouth" the word). Use the pictures below to help you. Your partner will decide which word you said by looking at the shape of your mouth.*

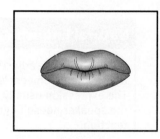 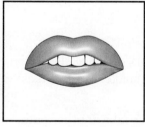 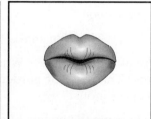

/p/, /b/   **/f/, /v/**   **/w/**

B | *PAIRS: Repeat the exercise in Part A. This time, say the words aloud.*

---

[1] wary: *careful;* [2] pest: *a bug or person that bothers you*

/p/ pie, /b/ buy, /f/ fine, /v/ vine, and /w/ wine   **77**

EXERCISE 6: Game: /p/, /b/, /f/, /v/, and /w/

Play this game in two teams—Team A and Team B. Give points for correct answers, pronounced correctly.

Team A: Ask the questions on page 202 to the players on Team B.
Team B: Answer the questions with a word that has a /p/, /b/, /f/, /v/, or /w/ sound. Then ask Team A
the questions on page 206.

EXAMPLE:

Team A: What's the opposite of *answer*?

Team B: *Question.*

STEP 3 COMMUNICATION PRACTICE

FEARS AND PHOBIAS

EXERCISE 7: Fears

A | *Listen to the conversation.*

MIKE: Watch out! There's a snake!

IVANA: You're afraid of snakes? What's so scary about snakes? That's a little garden snake. Most snakes aren't poisonous.

MIKE: They give me the creeps.[1] Let's take another path.

IVANA: OK, but watch out for spiders. They give me the creeps.

B | *PAIRS: Practice the conversation.*

> **Natural English**
>
> Use *What's so* + adjective + *about* to ask about someone's reaction. The expression usually means that the speaker doesn't agree with the reaction.
>
> *What's so scary* about snakes? Most of them aren't poisonous.
>
> *What's so scary* about spiders? Most of them are harmless.

---

[1] give . . . the creeps: *to scare*

EXERCISE 8: Phobias

A | *Listen and repeat. Make sure you understand the words.*

phobia	unreasonable	claustrophobic	string
panicky	gravity	eggshells	

B | *Listen to the recording and then answer the questions.*

1. What's a phobia?
2. What's a common phobia?
3. What are some rare phobias?

EXERCISE 9: Common Phobias

What are people afraid of? A poll[1] asked Americans about their phobias. Read the ten most common phobias in the chart.

Phobias	Rank	Do you have this phobia?
Cancer		
Confined spaces		
Death		
Flying		
Heights		
Open spaces		
People and social situations		
Spiders		
Thunderstorms		
Vomiting		

_____

[1] poll: *questionnaire that asks a lot of people the same questions in order to find out what they think about a subject*

A | *Rank the phobias from most common* **(1)** *to least common* **(10)**. *Then check* (✓) *the phobias you have.*

B | *PAIRS: Compare your rankings in Part A. (Then check your answers below.) Do you and your partner have similar phobias? Why do you think people have these phobias?*

STEP 4 EXTENDED PRACTICE

Accuracy Practice *Listen again to Exercises 1, 2, and 3 on pages 76 and 77. Then record the words.*

Fluency Practice *Record your answers to the questions.*

1. Do you have any of the phobias listed in Exercise 9?
2. What are you afraid of?
3. Are all the phobias in Exercise 9 unreasonable fears? Why or why not?

/s/ <u>s</u>even and /z/ <u>z</u>ero

The pictures show how to say /s/ and /z/.

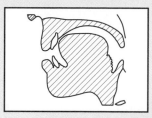 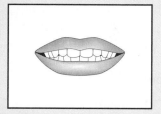

<u>s</u>even /s/

<u>z</u>ero /z/

The tip of your tongue is high in your mouth, behind your top teeth.

/s/ is voiceless.
/z/ is voiced.

Spellings for /s/	Spellings for /z/
Common *s* **s**ome, **s**i**s**ter, thi**s** *ss* me**ss**y, po**ss**ible, cla**ss** *se* hor**se**, mou**se**, promi**se**	**Common** *z, zz, ze* **z**oo, di**zz**y, si**ze** *s* between vowels: bu**s**y, ea**s**y, mu**s**ic *se* becau**se**, plea**se**, ri**se**

Other
c *(before e, i, y)* **c**ent, **c**ity,
  bi**c**ycle
sc **sc**ent, **sc**ience, **sc**issors
x (pronounced /ks/)
  e**x**cellent, e**x**ercise ne**x**t
Silent *s*: i**s**land, ai**s**le
	Other
	ss de**ss**ert, po**ss**ess, sci**ss**ors
	x (pronounced /gz/) e**x**am,
	  e**x**ample, e**x**actly

EXERCISE 1: Voiced /z/ and Voiceless /s/

a. Put your fingers against the side of your throat.

b. Make a long /zzzzzz/ and feel the vibrations (the voicing).

c. Make a long /ssssss/. You won't feel any vibration because /s/ is voiceless.

d. Alternate between /ssssss/ and /zzzzzz/ in the same breath. Feel the vibration turn off and on: /sssssszzzzzzssssssszzzzzzzsssssszzzzzz/.

e. Alternate between /asssa/ and /azzza/. Hold the /sss/ and /zzz/ as long as you can. Notice the difference.

EXERCISE 2: Words with /z/

A | *Listen and repeat the words.*

1. busy	**4.** business	**7.** crazy	**10.** was
2. dizzy	**5.** raisin	**8.** easy	**11.** wise
3. lazy	**6.** reason	**9.** result	**12.** noise

B | *PAIRS: Say the words. Take turns.*

EXERCISE 3: Listen for Differences: /z/ vs. /s/

A | *Listen and repeat the words.*

1. a. race	**4. a.** place	**7. a.** buses
b. raise	**b.** plays	**b.** buzzes
2. a. rice	**5. a.** loose	**8. a.** Miss
b. rise	**b.** lose	**b.** Ms.
3. a. advice	**6. a.** lacy	**9. a.** ice
b. advise	**b.** lazy	**b.** eyes

B | *Listen again and circle the words you hear.*

EXERCISE 4: Fill in the Grid

PAIRS: Each of you has a grid that is partially complete. Don't show your grid to your partner. Take turns asking each other for missing words. When you finish, compare your grids. They should be the same. Students A's grid is on page 203. Student B's grid is on page 206.

What's in box A2?

EXERCISE 5: Differences in Meaning

A | *Listen to the sentences.*

1. **a.** He <u>races</u> cows.   **b.** He <u>raises</u> cows.

2. **a.** Here's the <u>racer</u>.   **b.** Here's the <u>razor</u>.

3. **a.** The <u>bus</u> is too loud.   **b.** The <u>buzz</u> is too loud.

4. **a.** I like <u>Miss</u> Evans.   **b.** I like <u>Ms.</u> Evans.

5. **a.** He likes the <u>place</u>.   **b.** He likes the <u>plays</u>.

6. **a.** It's a great <u>price</u>.   **b.** It's a great <u>prize</u>.

B | *Listen again and circle the sentences you hear.*

C | *PAIRS: Use the sentences from Part A to make conversations. Pronounce /s/ and /z/ carefully. When you ask a question, your voice should rise at the end. Listen as your teacher reads the examples.*

EXAMPLES:

A: He races cows.

B: Did you say, "He raises cows?"

A: No. I said, "He races cows."

OR

A: He races cows.

B: Did you say, "He races cows?"

A: Yes, I did.

EXERCISE 6: Sounds and Grammar

Some words end in /s/ when they're nouns or adjectives and in /z/ when they're verbs. The vowel before /z/ is longer than the vowel before /s/.

A | *Listen and repeat the phrases.*

Noun/Adjective: /s/	Verb: /z/
1. a use	to use
2. an excuse	to excuse
3. the advice[1]	to advise[2]
4. a choice	to choose
5. a house	to house
6. a close friend	to close the door
7. a loose shirt	to lose something

B | *Complete each sentence with a word in parentheses.*

1. This three-story _____ can _____ three families.
   (hou**se** /s/, hou**se** /z/)

2. _____ carefully so that you make the right _____.
   (choi**ce** /s/, choo**se** /z/)

3. Give good _____ when you _____ your friends.
   (advi**ce** /s/, advi**se** /z/)

4. _____ me, I have a good _____ for being late.
   (excu**se** /s/, excu**se** /z/)

5. Don't _____ this phone. It's for office _____ only.
   (u**se** /s/, u**se** /z/)

C | *PAIRS: Practice the sentences. Pronounce the bold letters /s/ when the word is a noun or adjective. Pronounce the bold letters /z/ when the word is a verb.*

---

[1] advice: *(noun) an opinion you give someone about what he or she should do;* [2] advise: *(verb) to tell someone what you think he or she should do*

LIFE LESSONS AND OTHERS' ADVICE

EXERCISE 7: Advice

A | *Listen and repeat the conversation.*

ANNA: Bill Gates didn't take his parents' advice to stay in college and graduate from Harvard.

YOUNG: Why not?

ANNA: Paul Allen, the cofounder of Microsoft, needed his help. So Gates decided to drop out of school.

YOUNG: I wonder what would have happened if he'd followed his parents' advice?*

---

*Natural English

Notice the reduced pronunciation of the modal perfect *would have happened*.

I wonder what *woulda happened* if he'd followed his parents' advice?

B | *PAIRS: Each of you has a chart that is partially complete. Don't show your chart to your partner. Student A has information about situations that influenced Bill Gates's life and career. Student B has information about the lessons Gates learned from those situations. Take turns reading the information in your chart to your partner. Take notes to complete your chart (don't write everything your partner reads.) When you finish, compare your charts. The information should be the same. Student A's information is on page 203. Student B's information is on page 207.*

C | *PAIRS: In your opinion, what was the most important lesson Gates learned? Why?*

EXERCISE 8: Your Turn

A | *Use the lines to describe some advice that you got from someone or gave to someone. Was it good advice or bad advice? If the advice was taken, what was the result?*

_____

_____

_____

B | *PAIRS: Tell your partner about the advice you described.*

STEP 4 EXTENDED PRACTICE

Accuracy Practice *Listen again to Exercises 2A and 3A on page 82. Then record the words.*

Fluency Practice *Record your answers to the questions in Exercise 8A.*

UNIT 17 /ʃ/ <u>sh</u>oe and /ʒ/ televi<u>si</u>on

STEP 1 PRESENTATION

The pictures show how to say /ʃ/ and /ʒ/.

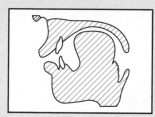 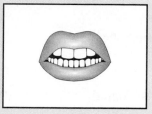

<u>sh</u>oe /ʃ/

televi<u>si</u>on /ʒ/

Pull the tip of your tongue back from the front of your mouth.
Round your lips a little.

/ʃ/ is voiceless.
/ʒ/ is voiced.

Spellings for /ʃ/	Spellings for /ʒ/
Common *sh* **sh**op, fa**sh**ion, wi**sh**	**Common** *si* deci**si**on, televi**si**on, vi**si**on
Other *ti* condi**ti**on, na**ti**on, pa**ti**ent *ci* musi**ci**an, so**ci**al, spe**ci**al *ssi* depre**ssi**on, discu**ssi**on, permi**ssi**on	**Other** *su* ca**su**al, plea**su**re, trea**su**re *ge* bei**ge**, gara**ge**, massa**ge**
Unusual ma**ch**ine, o**ce**an, **su**re, pre**ss**ure	**Unusual** a**zu**re[1]

---

[1] azure: *a light purplish shade of blue*

EXERCISE 1: Words with /ʃ/

🎧 *Listen and repeat the words.*

1. **sh**ine
2. **s**ugar
3. **sh**oe
4. **Ch**icago

5. gla**ci**er
6. spe**ci**al
7. rela**ti**on
8. vaca**ti**on

9. ca**sh**
10. fi**sh**
11. wi**sh**
12. pu**sh**

EXERCISE 2: Words with /ʒ/

🎧 *Listen and repeat the words.*

1. deci**si**on
2. plea**su**re
3. A**si**a
4. divi**si**on

5. u**su**al
6. occa**si**on
7. mea**su**re
8. bei**ge**

9. a**z**ure
10. televi**si**on
11. vi**si**on
12. gara**ge**

EXERCISE 3: Sounds and Spellings

🎧 **A** | *Listen and repeat the words.*

1. **s**uper
2. **s**ure
3. ca**s**ual
4. re**s**ult

5. vi**s**it
6. vi**s**ion
7. promi**s**ing
8. ea**s**ier

9. expan**s**ion
10. ra**c**ial
11. mou**s**e
12. mu**s**eum

13. mas**s**a**ge**
14. o**ce**an
15. ni**ce**
16. plea**s**ure

B | *How are the bold letters in Part A pronounced? Write each word in the correct column.*

/s/	/ʃ/	/z/	/ʒ/
super	_____	_____	_____
_____	_____	_____	_____
_____	_____	_____	_____
_____	_____	_____	_____

C | *PAIRS: Compare your answers. Then say the words in each column. Take turns.*

EXERCISE 4: Special and Usual

A | *Listen to the conversations and complete the sentences with the words you hear.*

1. **WAITER:**   Would you like to hear our _____ today?

   TOMÁS: Yes. Is there a _____ special?

2. **MATT:**   What are you doing this weekend?

   ANNA: Just _____ _____. Hanging out with friends.[1]

3. **SAMMY:**   Are we going to take another field trip[2] this semester?

   TEACHER: Sorry, Sammy. For the rest of the semester it's _____

   _____ _____.

4. **ANNA:**   I need to see a _____, someone who knows about skin. I

   have a red rash on my arm. It itches constantly.

   RECEPTIONIST: Oh, you mean a dermatologist. What kind of _____ do

   you have?

5. **ANNA:**   Why are you going to Miami for _____? What's so

   _____ about Miami?

   MICHAEL: Everything—the beaches, the food, the nightlife—everything.

Natural English

In the words *usual* and *usually*, the letters *su* can be pronounced in two ways:

usual /yúwʒwəl/ or /yúʒuwəl/

usually /yúwʒwəliy/ or /yúwʒuwəliy/

B | *PAIRS: Practice the conversations in Part A. Take turns.*

---

[1] hanging out with friends (informal): *spending time with friends;* [2] field trip: *an occasion when students go somewhere to learn about a particular subject*

TIME OFF

EXERCISE 5: Paid Time Off Around the World

A | *Listen to the recording. Then read the statements below. Write* **T (True)** *or* **F (False)** *next to each statement. Correct the false sentences.*

_____ **1.** U.S. workers get the least amount of paid time off, compared to other countries in the survey.

_____ **2.** Paid time off in the U.S. depends on the size of the company.

_____ **3.** Americans are able to rest and relax on vacation.

_____ **4.** In Finland, employers voluntarily give their employees longer vacations.

B | *PAIRS: Each of you has part of the information from the global survey on paid time off. Don't show your information to your partner. Complete the charts by sharing your information. Student A's information in on page 203. Student B's information is on page 207.*

EXERCISE 6: Vacations

A | *Listen to the words. The bold letters are pronounced /s/, /ʃ/, /z/, or /ʒ/.*

glaciers	massage	international food	azure water
fashionable people	relaxing	shopping	nutritious food
unusual people	adventure	champagne	shows
restful	sunshine	expensive	delicious food
inexpensive	museums	dangerous	boring

B | PAIRS: Read the vacations below. Find words in the box to describe these vacations and write them on the lines below. You can use the same words more than once, and you can add your own words.

1. salmon-fishing in Alaska

   _____

2. diving for buried treasure in the Caribbean

   _____

3. staying home, sleeping late, watching television

   _____

4. a week in New York City

   _____

5. two weeks at a health spa

   _____

6. a week in Paris

   _____

7. a week of race-car driving lessons

   _____

C | PAIRS: Answer the questions.

1. Have you ever taken any of the vacations listed in Part B?
2. Which of these vacations would you like to take and why?

STEP 4 EXTENDED PRACTICE

Accuracy Practice *Listen again to Exercises 1 and 2 on page 88. Then record the words.*

Fluency Practice *Record a description of a vacation you've taken. Where did you go? What did you do? Did you have a good time? Why or why not?*

/tʃ/ <u>ch</u>icken and /dʒ/ <u>j</u>acket

The pictures show how to say /tʃ/ and /dʒ/.

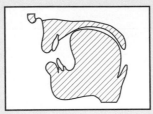 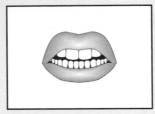

<u>ch</u>icken /tʃ/
<u>j</u>acket /dʒ/

The tip of your tongue is high and pulled back from your teeth.
Your lips are a little rounded.

/tʃ/ is voiceless.
/dʒ/ is voiced.

Note

Do you say *wash* when you mean *watch*? If this is a problem, be sure to start the
last sound in *watch* with a /t/. You will not hear the /t/ as a separate sound.

Spellings for /tʃ/	Spellings for /dʒ/
Common	**Common**
ch **ch**ance, **ch**icken, lun**ch**	*j* **j**azz, **J**uly, **j**ust
(In some words, ch has a	*ge* colle**ge**, **Ge**orge, stran**ge**
/k/ sound: *a**ch**e, **Ch**ristmas*.	*dge* bri**dge**, e**dge**, ju**dge**
In some words, ch has a	
/ʃ/ sound: *Chicago, machine*.)	
tch ki**tch**en, ma**tch**, wa**tch**	
Other	**Other**
tu fu**tu**re, na**tu**ral, pic**tu**re	*du* e**du**cation, gra**du**ate,
ti ques**ti**on	indivi**du**al
c **c**ello	*di* sol**di**er

EXERCISE 1: Words with /tʃ/ and /dʒ/

🎧 *Listen and repeat the words.*

/tʃ/			/dʒ/	
1. **ch**e**ck**	5. na**t**u**r**e	9. **j**a**zz**	13. pi**ge**on
2. **ch**alk	6. tea**ch**er	10. **j**a**ck**et	14. colle**ge**
3. **ch**eap	7. ca**tch**	11. **g**ym	15. a**ge**
4. ki**tch**en	8. su**ch**	12. refri**ge**rator	16. en**g**ine

EXERCISE 2: Listen for Differences

🎧 **A** | *Listen and repeat the words.*

1.	**a.** **ch**oice	4.	**a.** mu**sh**	7.	**a.** **ch**oke
	b. **J**oyce		**b.** mu**ch**		**b.** **j**oke
2.	**a.** e**dge**	5.	**a.** le**g**ion	8.	**a.** ca**sh**
	b. e**tch**		**b.** le**s**ion²		**b.** ca**tch**
3.	**a.** occa**s**ion	6.	**a.** H (/eytʃ/)	9.	**a.** ple**dg**er³
	b. a Ca**j**un¹		**b.** a**ge**		**b.** plea**s**ure

B | *PAIRS: Say a word from Part A. Your partner will tell you which word you said.*

EXERCISE 3: Fill in the Grid

PAIRS: Each of you has a grid that is partially complete. Don't show your grid to your partner. Take turns asking each other for missing words. When you finish, compare your grids. They should be the same. Students A's grid is on page 203. Student B's grid is on page 207.

What's in box A2?

---

¹ a Cajun: *a member of an ethnic group in Louisiana with a French background;* ² lesion: *a cut or injury to the skin;* ³ pledger: *someone who makes a promise*

EXERCISE 4: Joining Final Consonants

A | *Review the rules for joining final consonants.*

> **1.** Join final consonants to following vowels clearly.
>
> employment‿agency
>
> **2.** When a final consonant is followed by a different consonant, say the final consonant but keep it short (ᵎ). Then immediately say the next word.
>
> jobᵎ market

B | *Listen and repeat the phrases. Join words together correctly.*

Consonant + Vowel

1. a lar**ge**‿apartment
2. chan**ge**‿a dollar
3. How mu**ch**‿is it?
4. wa**tch**‿a movie

Consonant + Consonant

5. a**ge**ᵎ limit
6. lun**ch**ᵎ break
7. stran**ge**ᵎ noises
8. whi**ch**ᵎ one

EXERCISE 5: Conversations

A | *Listen to the questions. Then listen to the responses.*

Questions

_____ **1.** How long is your lun**ch** break?

_____ **2.** Whi**ch** one do you want?

_____ **3.** Are there any lar**ge** apartments?

_____ **4.** Can you **ch**ange a 50-dollar bill?

_____ **5.** How mu**ch** is that cou**ch**?

_____ **6.** Do you want to wa**tch** a movie?

_____ **7.** Is there an a**ge** limit?

_____ **8.** Did you hear a stran**ge** noise?

Responses

a. Yes. But the rent is more.

b. A thousand dollars.

c. Just an hour.

d. Yes. You have to be 21.

e. No, thanks. I have a headache.

f. The lar**ge** one.

g. It's **j**ust the dog outside.

h. Sorry. I don't have that mu**ch**.

B | *PAIRS: Match the questions and responses. Then practice the conversations.*

CHANGING JOBS

EXERCISE 6: Career Change

A | *Listen to the conversation.*

SONIA: Nick finally decided to leave the Marines.

TONY: I'll bet your sister is happy about that. How does he feel about it?

SONIA: Well, he knows it's the right decision. He wants to be home to help raise his son.

TONY: What's he going to do now?

SONIA: He met with a headhunter[1] that specializes in finding civilian jobs[2] for ex-officers. It turns out that officers have skills that civilian employers want.

TONY: Like what?

SONIA: Well, they have leadership experience. They're used to making decisions quickly and calmly under pressure. But they're also used to a chain of command, taking orders from superior officers.*

TONY: I never thought of it that way. Those are valuable skills.

---

*Natural English

Pronounce *used to* as one word: /yuwstə/ or /yuwstuw/.

Use *be used to* + gerund/noun to show that something is so routine that it is easy for you. The expression means "be accustomed to doing something." The main verb is *be*, and it can be used in any tense.

> They're /yuwstə/ making decisions quickly and calmly under pressure.

> They're /yuwstə/ taking orders from superior officers.

B | *PAIRS: Practice the conversation in Part A. Take turns.*

---

[1] headhunter: *someone who finds people with the right skills and experience to do a particular job;*
[2] civilian jobs: *non-military jobs*

/tʃ/ <u>ch</u>icken and /dʒ/ <u>j</u>acket **95**

EXERCISE 7: Jobs

A | *Listen and repeat the jobs.*

1. bu**tch**er _____

2. engineer _____

3. forest ranger _____

4. **j**azz pianist _____

5. **judge** _____

6. sol**dier** _____

7. store mana**g**er _____

8. tea**ch**er _____

9. travel a**g**ent _____

10. wa**tch**maker _____

B | *Read the job characteristics below. What characteristics describe the jobs in Part A? Write the characteristics on the lines, using your own words or those below.*

Requires specialized skills/talents—Requires general skills

Common job—Unusual job

Dangerous/exciting—Routine/boring

Indoor work—Outdoor work

Competitive/risky—Less competitive/more secure

Well paid—Not (very) well paid

C | *GROUPS: Compare the characteristics you chose for the jobs in Part A. What are the two best jobs on the list? The two worst jobs? Why?*

STEP 4 EXTENDED PRACTICE

Accuracy Practice *Listen again to Exercises 1 and 2A on page 93. Then record the words.*

Fluency Practice *Record a description of the job you have or one that you'd like to have. What do you like about the job? What don't you like?*

UNIT 19 -*S* Endings: Plurals, Possessives, and Present Tense

STEP 1 PRESENTATION

-*S* endings can be pronounced as a syllable or a sound.

1. Pronounce the **-*s*** ending as a new syllable (/əz/ or /ɪz/) when the base word ends in an *s*-like sound (/s, z, ʃ, ʒ, tʃ, dʒ/).

    one boss → two bosses

2. Pronounce the -*s* ending /s/ or /z/ when the base word does not end in an *s*-like sound.

    a. Use /s/ when the base word ends in /p, t, k, θ, f/.

    one student → two students
         /t/   /ts/

    b. Use /z/ when the base word ends in a vowel sound or /b, d, g, ð, v, m, n, ŋ, r, l/.

    end → It ends at 8:00 P.M.
    /d/   /dz/

Use -*s* endings for:

1. Plural nouns: two boys, four books
2. Present tense (third-person singular): She plays the piano.
3. Possessives: my mother's house
4. Contractions of *is* or *has*: John's late.

Notes

1. Many nouns that end in /f/ change /f/ to /v/ in the plural. The plural ending is pronounced /z/.

    half → halves   knife → knives

2. Some nouns that end in /f/ have verbs that end in /v/. Pronounce the present ending /z/ if the verb ends in /v/. Pronounce the present ending /s/ if the verb ends in /f/.

    he believes (noun: *belief*)   he proves (noun: *proof*)

3. Native speakers may drop /θ/ when it is followed by plural -*s*. They may lengthen the plural /s/ to hold the place of /θ/.

    month → months /mənts/   fifth → fifths /fɪfθs/ or /fɪfs/   clothes → (to) close

4. Many speakers drop /ð/ before the plural ending /z/ and make the ending a long /z/.

    bathe → bathes /beyðz/ or /beyz/   breathe → breathes /briyðz/ or /briyz/

EXERCISE 1: Listen for Syllables: -S endings

🎧 *Listen and repeat the words. Underline each syllable in the plural words. Pronounce the ending as a new syllable.*

1. **a.** box
   b. boxes

2. **a.** catch
   b. catches

3. **a.** wish
   b. wishes

4. **a.** dress
   b. dresses

5. **a.** rose
   b. roses

6. **a.** choice
   b. choices

7. **a.** pass
   b. passes

8. **a.** kiss
   b. kisses

9. **a.** age
   b. ages

EXERCISE 2: How Does It Sound?

🎧 **A** | *Listen to the nouns. Write the plural noun in the middle column. If the plural ending is pronounced /əz/ or /ɪz/, write **syllable** in the right column. If the plural ending is a final sound, write **sound**.*

	Plural	Syllable or Sound?
1. book	books	sound
2. exercise		
3. hat		
4. leaf		
5. month		
6. mother		
7. prize		
8. sandwich		
9. smile		
10. window		

B | *PAIRS: Compare your answers. Then practice saying the plural nouns.*

EXERCISE 3: Identical Twins

A | *Read the phrases. Then listen to the descriptions of Bruno and Marko Kistler. Check (✓) the information you hear about the brothers.*

	Bruno	Marko
1. have dark, curly hair	✓	✓
2. have short hair	____	____
3. spend more time on sports	____	____
4. dance	____	____
5. play the guitar	____	____
6. married	____	____
7. have a daughter	____	____
8. have a girlfriend	____	____
9. work long hours	____	____
10. does gardening work	____	____

B | *PAIRS: Compare your answers. Then take turns describing the brothers. Use **-s** endings when necessary. Follow the example.*

EXAMPLE: Bruno and Marko both have dark, curly hair.

EXERCISE 4: Family and Friends

A | *Listen to the recording and complete the sentences with the words you hear.*

1. My father _____ in Mexico City.

2. His name is Alberto but everyone _____ him Beto.

3. He _____ in a bank as a loan officer.

4. In his free time, he _____ to paint, especially pictures of my mother.

5. She _____ him to stop because she already _____ 50 large

   portraits.

B | *PAIRS: Tell your partner about a friend or family member. Use present verbs with **-s** endings when you can.*

TIME MANAGEMENT

EXERCISE 5: Hurrying

A | *Listen to the conversation.*

ALIYA: Do you want to go for coffee?

TAKU: Sure. Where's Amir running off to?[1]

ALIYA: The library. He says he's got to study.

TAKU: But it's Friday. He has the whole weekend to study.

ALIYA: Not really. He works on the weekend. And he has a family. He's under a lot of pressure.

TAKU: Still, he's got to take some time for himself, to relax.

Natural English

Use the contractions *'ve* or *'s* in the expression *have got to*. The last two words, *got to*, are usually pronounced as one word: *gotta*.

I*'ve gotta* go.

He*'s gotta* take some time for himself.

B | *PAIRS: Practice the conversation. Take turns.*

C | *GROUPS: Answer the questions in small groups.*

1. The Chinese philosopher Lao Tzu once said, "Nature does not hurry, yet everything is accomplished." What do you think this quote means?

2. Do you have enough to time to do everything you want to do? Explain.

3. Is it possible for you to get everything done without hurrying?

---

[1] run off to: *to hurry to*

EXERCISE 6: Your Turn

A | *How do you spend your time? Read the activities in the left column of the chart. How much time do you spend doing these activities? Write the minutes or hours per day or week next to each activity in the right column. Then use the blank rows to write other activities.*

Activities	Time Spent on Activity (minutes or hours/day or week)
School or job:	
classes	
studying	
work/internship	
transportation (to and from work, school, etc.)	
family commitments	
Personal needs:	
sleeping	
eating/preparing meals	
exercise/sports	
personal care (taking a shower, getting dressed, etc.)	
Free time:	
relaxing alone (watching TV, playing video games, reading, hobbies)	
socializing with friends or family, entertainment	

B | *PAIRS: Compare your charts from Part A.*

C | *PAIRS: Look at your partner's chart. Choose three activities that take up a lot of your partner's time. Tell the class about your partner. Be sure to use the -s ending with present, singular verbs.*

STEP 4 EXTENDED PRACTICE

Accuracy Practice *Listen again to Exercises 1 and 2A on page 98. Then record the words.*

Fluency Practice *Record your answers to the questions.*

1. Do you think you're an organized person?
2. What would you like to spend more time doing? Why?
3. What would you like to spend less time doing? Why?

20 /r/ _right and /l/ _light

STEP 1 PRESENTATION

The pictures show how to say /r/ and /l/.

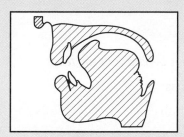

_right, _road /r/

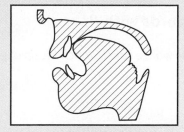

_light, _left /l/

Start with the tip of your tongue turned up and back. Then lower the tip of your tongue.
When you lower the tip of your tongue, do not touch the top of your mouth.

Touch the tip of your tongue just behind the top teeth.

Notes

1. /r/ is a "movement" sound: The tongue moves out of a turned-back position. It does not touch the top of the mouth.

2. /l/ is a "contact" sound: The tip of the tongue touches behind the top teeth.

Spellings for /r/ and /l/

Common
/r/ and /l/ are usually spelled with the letters, *r* and *l*.

Other
Silent *l*:
wa*l*k, ta*l*k, cha*l*k, ha*l*f, cou*l*d, shou*l*d, ca*l*m, sa*l*mon

EXERCISE 1: Words with /r/

🎧 *Listen and repeat the words. For /r/, start with the tip of your tongue turned up and back. Lower the tip of your tongue. Do not let the tip of your tongue touch the top of your mouth as it lowers.*

1. right	**4.** ready	**7.** grass
2. red	**5.** sorry	**8.** crime
3. room	**6.** arrive	**9.** try

EXERCISE 2: Words with /l/

🎧 *Listen and repeat the words. For /l/, touch the tip of your tongue behind your top teeth.*

1. listen	**4.** alive	**7.** glass
2. long	**5.** a lot	**8.** climb
3. love	**6.** collect	**9.** fly

EXERCISE 3: Listen for Differences: /r/ vs. /l/

🎧 **A |** *Listen and repeat the words.*

1. a. lay	**4. a.** list	**7. a.** collect
b. Ray	**b.** wrist	**b.** correct
2. a. Willy	**5. a.** glass	**8. a.** light
b. weary	**b.** grass	**b.** right
3. a. alive	**6. a.** climb	**9. a.** loyal[1]
b. arrive	**b.** crime	**b.** royal[2]

🎧 **B |** *Listen again and circle the words you hear.*

C | *PAIRS: Say a word from Part A. Your partner will tell you which word you said.*

---

[1] loyal: *always supporting a particular person, set of beliefs, or country;* [2] royal: *relating to or belonging to a king or queen*

EXERCISE 4: Differences in Meaning

A | *Listen to the sentences and responses.*

Sentences	**Responses**
1. a. There's <u>grass</u> on the floor.	I probably brought it in when I was outside.
b. There's <u>glass</u> on the floor.	The window broke.
2. a. It was a terrible <u>crime</u>.	Did the police catch the criminal?
b. It was a terrible <u>climb</u>.	I agree. Hiking in the rain isn't fun.
3. a. Your answer is <u>wrong</u>.	I think it's correct.
b. Your answer is <u>long</u>.	No. Yours is short.
4. a. The teacher <u>collected</u> the tests.	She didn't get mine.
b. The teacher <u>corrected</u> the tests.	How did you do?

B | *PAIRS: Choose a sentence from Part A. Pronounce the underlined word carefully so your partner can say the correct response.*

EXERCISE 5: Words with /r/ and /l/

A | *Listen and repeat the words.*

1. really	**5.** electricity	**9.** parallel
2. slippery	**6.** laboratory	**10.** realistic
3. salary	**7.** relatives	**11.** military
4. library	**8.** liberate	**12.** celebrate

B | *PAIRS: Practice saying the words. Take turns.*

EXERCISE 6: Sentences Full of Sounds

A | *Listen and repeat the sentences.*

1. We celebrated after the military liberated the city.
2. Do librarians really make good salaries?
3. Most people are loyal to the royal family.
4. I like the bright orange of carrots and the light green of celery.

B | *Choose a sentence and say it to the class.*

GOING PLACES

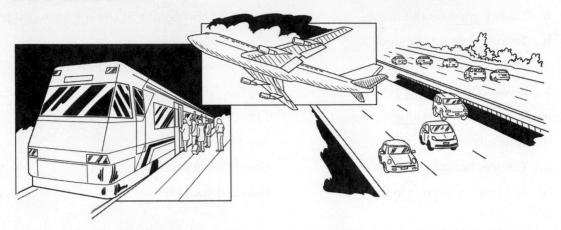

EXERCISE 7: Around the World

A | *Listen to the conversation.*

RICARDO: I'd like to visit a country on every continent in the world.

LISA: Even Antarctica?

RICARDO: Yes, but that's probably last on my list.

LISA: That's a really ambitious plan.

RICARDO: Yes, but I like to travel.

B | *PAIRS: Practice the conversation. Then tell your partner about the countries and continents you've visited.*

Natural English

Notice the difference in meaning between *like* and *'d like*.

I *like* to travel. = I enjoy traveling.

I'*d like* to travel. = I want to travel.

Use the contraction *I'd like* when you speak. Pronounce /d/ but keep it short. Say *like* immediately. Don't separate the contraction and *like*.

I'd like to visit every continent in the world.

EXERCISE 8: Destinations

A | *GROUPS: List as many countries as you can on the lines below that have /r/ or /l/ in their names.*

Europe	Asia	Africa	North America	South America
France	Korea	Morocco	Costa Rica	Colombia

B | *GROUPS: Choose a country that you'd like to visit and explain why you'd like to go there. You can use your own words or phrases or those below. Start this way: "I'd like to go to ____."*

1. adventure
2. beautiful scenery
3. culturally rich
4. delicious food
5. friendly people

6. great weather
7. historical place(s)
8. interesting place(s)
9. island(s), rivers, lakes
10. lots of things to do

EXERCISE 9: The Confusing Town of Logan

A | *First look at the street map of Logan. Then listen and repeat the sentences.*

1. Logan Road is the main road in the town of Logan.
2. Logan Road runs north and south.
3. Rocket Road and Locket Road run east and west.
4. Grassy Lane and Glassy Lane run north and south.
5. Myra's Drive and Myla's Drive also run north and south.
6. There are 12 businesses on Grassy Lane, Glassy Lane, Myra's Drive, and Myla's Drive.

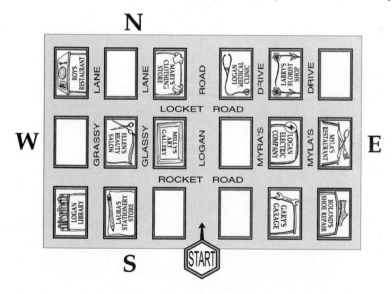

B | *PAIRS: Choose a place in Logan, but don't tell your partner the name of the place. Give your partner directions to the place. Pronounce /r/ and /l/ carefully. Follow the example.*

EXAMPLE:

STUDENT A: Go north on Logan Road. Turn right on Locket Road. Then turn left on Myla's Drive. Where are you?

STUDENT B: I'm at Larry's Florist Shop.

STEP 4 EXTENDED PRACTICE

🎧 🎤 **Accuracy Practice** *Listen again to Exercises 1, 2, and 3A on page 104. Then record the words.*

🎤 **Fluency Practice** *Record your answers to the questions.*

1. What are some countries that you'd like to visit? Why?
2. What are some countries that you wouldn't like to visit? Why?

UNIT 21 /m/ <u>m</u>ouse, /n/ <u>n</u>ose, and /ŋ/ si<u>ng</u>

STEP 1 PRESENTATION

The pictures show how to say /m/, /n/, and /ŋ/. These sounds are called nasal (nose) sounds because the air goes out through the nose.

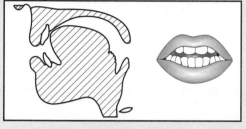
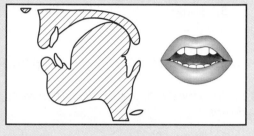

<u>m</u>ouse, ho<u>m</u>e /m/

Close your lips.

<u>n</u>ose, <u>n</u>i<u>n</u>e /n/

Touch the tip of your tongue behind the top teeth.

si<u>ng</u>, lo<u>ng</u> /ŋ/

Raise the back of your tongue. The tip of your tongue is in the bottom of your mouth.

Notes

1. In words that end in the letters -*ng*, there is no /g/ sound. For example, *sing* does not have a /g/ sound. In many words with *ng* spellings in the middle of the word, *g* is not pronounced. In some words, such as *finger*, the letter *g* is pronounced as /g/.

2. Adjectives that end in /ŋ/ add /g/ in the comparative and superlative: *long* /ŋ/, *longer* /ŋg/, *longest* /ŋg/.

3. Pronounce nasal consonants clearly when they end words. In some languages, nasal consonants after vowels "nasalize" the vowel, and the nasal consonant can be dropped. In English, however, nasal consonants must be clearly pronounced.

4. Join final nasal consonants to following vowels.

   hum a song   run away   sing out loud

Spellings for /m/	Spellings for /n/	Spellings for /ŋ/
Common *m* **m**ouse, s**m**all, **M**o**m** *mm* su**mm**er	**Common** *n* **n**ose, s**n**ake, **n**o**n**e *nn* su**nn**y	**Common** *ng* si**ng**, ri**ng**ing, wro**ng** *n* before *g, k*: E**n**glish, a**n**gry, ba**n**k, thi**n**k

Other
mn (silent *n*) autum~~n~~,
   hym~~n~~
	Other
	kn (silent *k*) ~~k~~now, ~~k~~nee,
	   ~~k~~nife
	gn (silent *g*) forei**g**n, si**g**n	

EXERCISE 1: Words with Nasal Consonants

🎧 *Listen and repeat the words.*

/m/	/n/	/ŋ/	/ŋg/, /ŋk/
1. most	6. nail	11. sing	16. younger
2. messy	7. necessary	12. wrong	17. angry
3. stomach	8. friendly	13. ring	18. longer
4. home	9. happen	14. hanging	19. drink
5. some	10. done	15. young	20. bank

EXERCISE 2: Sounds and Spelling

🎧 *Listen to the words and phrases. Then write **yes** in the blank if you hear a /g/ sound. Write **no** if you do not.*

1. sang __no__

2. longer _____

3. ringing _____

4. strongest _____

5. a strong army _____

6. hang it up _____

7. linger[1] _____

8. young _____

9. belonging _____

EXERCISE 3: Bingo

🎧 **A** | *Listen and repeat the words on the Bingo card.*

1. ring	6. Tim	11. Jan	16. sinner
2. hang	7. sung	12. king	17. simmer[4]
3. kin[2]	8. jam	13. singer	18. sun
4. bang	9. Kim	14. some	19. Bam!
5. rim[3]	10. ban	15. tin	20. ham

🎧 **B** | *Now play Bingo. Use the card in Part A. Listen carefully and cross out the words you hear. When you've crossed out a complete row or column, say "Bingo!"*

---

[1] linger: *to stay longer;* [2] kin: *a relative;* [3] rim: *edge;* [4] simmer: *to boil gently*

EXERCISE 4: Final Consonants

A | *Listen and write the word you hear in the blanks.*

1. Let's leave after the guests have _____ (sung/some).

2. They found _____ (Tim/tin) in the mountains.

3. Did you say "_____" (hang/ham)?

4. I think that's _____ (wrong/Ron).

B | *PAIRS: Choose a sentence and complete it with one of the words in parentheses. Your partner will tell you which word you said. Take turns.*

STEP 3 COMMUNICATION PRACTICE

FREE TIME

EXERCISE 5: We Could Go Hiking

A | *Listen and repeat the conversation. Pronounce nasal consonants clearly. Group words together and speak smoothly.*

MOTHER: We're all going to the park on Sunday.
Do you want to come?

MARK: Thanks, Mom, but I'm training on Sunday.
Remember, the marathon's[1] in two months.

MOTHER: Well, how about Saturday? We could go hiking.*

MARK: I don't think so. The running club's
meeting on Saturday.

B | *PAIRS: Practice the conversation. Take turns.*

> ### *Natural English
>
> Use *go* + verb + *ing* to describe activities that are fun. Stress the following verb more than *go*.
>
> We could *go híking*.
>
> Let's *go swímming*.
>
> I *went shópping*.
>
> For team or pair sports, use the verb *play*.
>
> Let's play basketball.
>
> Let's play tennis.

---

[1] marathon: *a 26.2 mile (42.2 km) race*

EXERCISE 6: Your Turn

A | *How do you spend your free time? Check (✓) the activities in the list that you like to do. Then write three more activities in the blanks.*

I spend my free time . . .

_____ **1.** watching TV

_____ **2.** cooking

_____ **3.** with my friends

_____ **4.** playing sports or exercising

_____ **5.** reading

_____ **6.** listening to music

_____ **7.** _____

_____ **8.** _____

_____ **9.** _____

B | *PAIRS: Compare your lists. Do you enjoy the same activities?*

STEP 4 EXTENDED PRACTICE

Accuracy Practice *Listen again to Exercises 1 and 2 on page 110. Then record the words.*

Fluency Practice *Record your answers to the questions.*

1. How do you spend your free time?
2. How do people in your country like to spend their free time?

STEP 1 PRESENTATION

The pictures show how to say /y/ and /dʒ/.

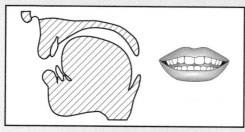

yet, you /y/

The center of your tongue slides up toward the front of your mouth.

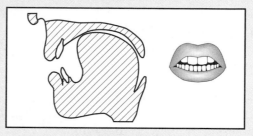

jet, general /dʒ/

Keep the tip of your tongue high and pulled back in your mouth. The lips protrude slightly. /dʒ/ starts with a /d/ sound.

Notes

1. /y/ is the second sound in several consonant clusters (consonant groups). The /y/ sound is usually not written in consonant clusters. When the vowel following these clusters is unstressed, it's pronounced /ə/.

   ré**gu**lar /gyə/   partí**cu**lar /kyə/   vocá**bu**lary /byə/   pó**pu**lar /pyə/

2. /y/ is the last sound of several vowels.

   m**y** /ay/   enj**oy** /oy/   s**ee** /iy/   s**ay** /ey/

   When these vowels are followed by another vowel, join /y/ to the next vowel.

   my uncle   enjoy it   see ʸit   say it

3. If your native language is Spanish, you may pronounce *yet* like *jet*. If this is a problem, start /y/ words with a long vowel: *iiiiiiés* (yes).

4. Some students pronounce *year* like *ear* and *yield* like *"eeled."* If this is a problem, try these tips:

   Start the word with a long vowel: *iiiiiéar.*

   Slide your tongue forward when you say these words.

Spellings for /y/	Spellings for /dʒ/
Common *y* **y**ellow, **y**ard, **y**awn, be**y**ond	See Unit 18.
Other *u* (at the beginning of some words) **u**se, **u**nion, **u**niversity *i* (after *n* and *l* if *i* is unstressed) conven**i**ent, famil**i**ar, mill**i**on *ew, iew, eau* (pronounced /yuw/) f**ew**, v**iew**, b**eau**tiful	

STEP 2 FOCUSED PRACTICE

EXERCISE 1: Words with /y/

🎧 *Listen and repeat the words.*

1. year	**5.** beyond	**9.** university
2. united	**6.** usual	**10.** useful
3. yell	**7.** yesterday	**11.** yolk
4. youth	**8.** young	**12.** yogurt

EXERCISE 2: Listen for Differences

🎧 **A** | *Listen and repeat the words.*

1. a. yes	**4. a.** yawn	**7. a.** yellow
b. Jess	**b.** John	**b.** Jell-O™
2. a. yolk	**5. a.** yam¹	**8. a.** use (noun)
b. joke	**b.** jam	**b.** juice
3. a. yet	**6. a.** Yale	**9. a.** year
b. jet	**b.** jail	**b.** ear

B | *PAIRS: Say a word from Part A. Your partner will tell you which word you said.*

EXERCISE 3: Consonant Clusters

🎧 *The bold letters in the words below are consonant clusters with /y/. Listen and repeat the words.*

1. com**pu**ter	**5.** **mu**sic	**9.** voca**bu**lary
2. **Hou**ston	**6.** parti**cu**lar	**10.** **beau**tiful
3. inter**view**	**7.** pe**cu**liar	**11.** re**gu**lar
4. opi**ni**on	**8.** po**pu**lation	**12.** fi**gu**re

---

¹ yam: *a sweet potato*

EXERCISE 4: Sentences Full of Sounds

A | *Listen to the sentences.*

1. You can't go to Yale if you're in jail.
2. The irregular shapes are particularly peculiar.
3. After the accident, he couldn't hear out of his left ear for a year.
4. I figured out how to fix the computer yesterday.
5. Yellow Jell-O™ usually has a lemon flavor.
6. Yes, Jess made John yawn.
7. The popular musician gave an interview about his career.
8. He used young jungle animals in his film this year.
9. If you go to the store, I could use some juice, yams, jam, and yeast.[1]

B | *Choose a sentence and say it to the class.*

STEP 3 COMMUNICATION PRACTICE

CONNECTED

EXERCISE 5: Growth of the Internet

A | *PAIRS: Read the quote. Then talk about what it means.*

Bill Clinton, president of the United States from 1993 to 2001, once said, "When I took office, only high-energy physicists had ever heard of what is called the World Wide Web . . . now even my cat has its own (web) page."

B | *Listen. Make sure you understand the words.*

physicists	estimated	blogs	exploded	100-fold increase[2]	arrange

---

[1] yeast: *a cooking bacteria that makes bread rise;* [2] 100-fold increase: *an increase of 100 times*

C | *Listen to the recording and then answer the questions.*

1. How many Internet users were there in 1995? _____

2. How many Internet users were there in 2010? _____

3. Describe the changes the Internet has made in:

news: _____

education: _____

social lives: _____

EXERCISE 6: Your Turn

Natural English

The word *to* has a very short pronunciation before consonants.

A: Do you use computers tə meet people?

B: No. I prefer tə meet people through friends.

PAIRS: Find out how your partner uses computers. Ask your partner the questions.

1. Do you use computers . . . ?

   a. for social networking
   b. for email
   c. to meet people (for example, online dating services)
   d. to listen to music
   e. to watch movies
   f. for banking
   g. for booking tickets

   h. for investing
   i. to take courses
   j. to play games
   k. for art/design
   l. for research/information
   m. for shopping
   n. other

2. Does the Internet save you time? Why or why not?

   _____

3. How dependent are you on technology? Explain.

   _____

STEP 4 EXTENDED PRACTICE

Accuracy Practice *Listen again to Exercises 1, 2A, and 3 on page 114. Then record the words.*

Fluency Practice *Record your answers to the questions.*

1. What do you think of Internet dating services? Explain.
2. Have you ever gone on a date arranged by an Internet dating service? If so, describe what happened.

/h/ <u>h</u>at; Reduction of *H* Words

The picture shows how to say /h/.

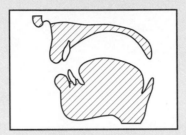

<u>h</u>at, a<u>h</u>ead /h/

/h/ is similar to the sound of breathing after exercise.

The back of your tongue should not be close to the top of your mouth.

Notes

1. The letter *h* is never pronounced at the beginning of some words. Use the article *an* with these words.

    an ̶hour   an ̶honest man   an ̶honor

    The letter *h* is also not pronounced in these words.

    ex̶haust   ex̶hibit   ve̶hicle

2. /h/ is often dropped in *he, him, his, her, have, has,* and *had* when they're unstressed inside a sentence. When *h* is "dropped," the rest of the word joins to the preceding word. If it's difficult for you to pronounce these reductions and join the words together, you can pronounce the words with /h/.

    What did ̶he give ̶her? (say "What diddy giver?")

3. /h/ is never dropped when *he, him, his, her, have, has,* and *had* begin a sentence. /h/ is never dropped in short answers with *have, has,* or *had*.

Have you met your new neighbor?

Yes, I have. Her name is Joan.

<table>
<tr><td colspan="1">Spellings for /h/</td></tr>
</table>

Common
h **h**ungry, **h**eart, **h**old, in**h**erit
Other
wh **wh**o, **wh**ose, **wh**om, **wh**ole
Silent *h*:
h̶our, h̶onest, h̶onor, h̶eir, h̶erb, veh̶icle, exh̶austed, exh̶ibit

STEP 2 FOCUSED PRACTICE

EXERCISE 1: Words with /h/

Listen and repeat the words.

1. happen	**4.** hostile	**7.** overhear	**10.** inhale
2. healthy	**5.** hint	**8.** uphill	**11.** ahead
3. harsh	**6.** human	**9.** behind	**12.** inhabit

EXERCISE 2: Sounds and Spelling

Listen and repeat the words. Draw a line through the letter **h** if it is not pronounced.

1. h̶our	**5.** heavy	**9.** unhappy	**13.** vehicle
2. head	**6.** behind	**10.** alcohol	**14.** hot
3. humid	**7.** honesty	**11.** honorable	**15.** however
4. hand	**8.** inherit	**12.** behave	**16.** heir

EXERCISE 3: Differences in Meaning

A | Listen to the sentences and responses.

Sentences	**Responses**
1. a. I <u>ate</u> ice cream.	You'll never lose weight eating that way!
b. I <u>hate</u> ice cream.	Really? Most people love it.
2. a. Do you use <u>hairspray</u>?	No, it makes my hair sticky.
b. Do you use <u>air spray</u>?	No, I just open a window.
3. a. Did you hear that <u>howl</u>?	Yes, there must be coyotes around.
b. Did you hear that <u>owl</u>?	Yes, it lives in the big tree beside the house.

(continued on next page)

Sentences	Responses

4. **a.** Did the <u>heart</u> organization put out this information?

Yes. It urges people to eat less fat and exercise regularly.

   b. Did the <u>art</u> organization put out this information?

Yes. It describes the new exhibit at the museum.

5. **a.** Please <u>eat</u> up the chicken.

I can't. I'm allergic[1] to it.

   b. Please <u>heat</u> up the chicken.

It's supposed to be served cold.

B | *PAIRS: Choose a sentence from Part A. Pronounce the underlined word carefully so your partner can say the correct response.*

EXERCISE 4: Reductions of *H* Words

🎧 *Listen and repeat the sentences. Pronounce the underlined words as one word. Do not pronounce* h.

1. What did he do? (say "diddy")

2. What's his name? (say "whatsız")

3. Where has he gone? (say "wherəziy")

4. Watch her. (say "watcher")

5. Look him in the eye. (say "lookım")

6. What have you done? (say "whatəv")

> ### Natural English
>
> When /h/ is dropped from pronouns, homonyms can be created.
>
> Watch her sounds like "watcher."
>
> You'll understand English better if you're familiar with these pronunciations. If it's difficult for you to join these words together, you can use the full forms of the words.
>
> Watch her.

EXERCISE 5: Sounds Like . . .

🎧 **A** | *Homophrases are two phrases that sound the same but have different spellings and meanings. Listen and repeat the phrases.*

1. Did you say *catcher*? _Did you say "catch her"?_____

2. Izzy Cumming? _____

3. canny[2] driver? _____

4. Oliver Boots _____

5. the delays of Koster Munny _____

6. The actresses left. _____

B | *PAIRS: Take turns saying each phrase. Then work with your partner to think of a phrase with **he**, **his**, **him**, **her**, **have**, **has**, or **had** that sounds the same (or nearly the same) and write it in the blank. Hints: A -y ending could be **he**; an -er ending could be **her**; an -es ending could be **has**; and of could be **have**. (Then check your answers on page 122.)*

---

[1] allergic (to something): *to have a condition that makes you sick when you eat, touch, or breathe a particular thing;* [2] canny: *smart and careful*

WEATHER

EXERCISE 6: Weather Conditions

A | *Listen and repeat. Make sure you understand the words.*

high heat	downpour	blizzard	thunder and lightning
breezy	drizzle	high humidity	tornado
calm	fair	high winds	shower
cool	hail	hurricane	warm

B | *PAIRS: Do the words in the box describe extreme weather conditions or mild weather conditions? Write the words from the box in the correct columns.*

Extreme Weather

high heat

_____

_____

_____

_____

_____

_____

_____

Mild Weather

_____

_____

_____

_____

_____

_____

EXERCISE 7: Find Someone Who . . .

*GROUPS: Work in large groups. Ask your classmates if they've experienced the weather listed in the chart. Write the names of classmates who answer **yes** in the right column.*

EXAMPLES:
Have you ever been in a hurricane?
Do you like heat and humidity?

Find someone who . . .	Names
has been in a hurricane, cyclone, typhoon, blizzard, etc.	
likes heat and humidity	
likes high heat but low humidity	
likes cold winters with lots of snow	
prefers four different seasons	
prefers year-round mild temperatures	
likes to watch weather reports or the weather channel	
thinks storms are exciting	

STEP 4 EXTENDED PRACTICE

Accuracy Practice *Listen again to Exercises 2 and 4 on pages 119 and 120. Then record them. When you record Exercise 4, join the underlined words together.*

Fluency Practice *Record a description of your ideal climate.*

EXERCISE 5B: 1. Did you say "catch her"? 2. Is he coming? 3. Can he drive her? 4. all of her boots 5. The delays have cost her money. 6. The actress has left.

UNIT 24 | Beginning Consonant Clusters

STEP 1 PRESENTATION

Pronounce the consonants in consonant clusters (groups of consonants) closely together. Don't separate them with a vowel sound.

1. **Clusters with /s/**

   spot   **sm**all   **sw**ing

   slow   **str**ong   **scr**eam

2. **Clusters with /r/ and /l/**

   pressure   **bl**ue   **thr**ee   **cl**imb   **gr**ow   **sl**eep

3. **Clusters with /w/**

   twelve   **dw**ell   **qu**ick   **Gw**en   **sw**ear   **qu**estion

4. **Clusters Inside Words**

   in**cr**ease   re**sp**ect   re**qu**est

5. **Rare Consonant Clusters**

   shrink /ʃr/   **shr**ivel   **shr**ub   **sph**ere /sf/

Notes

1. If your native language is Spanish, make sure you don't add a short /ɛ/ sound before /s/ clusters. If this is a problem, practice /s/ clusters by making a long /sssssss/ and then pronouncing the rest of the word: *ssstate*.

   state (not "estate")   steam (not "esteem")

2. If your native language is Korean, you may not pronounce the /w/ sound in /kw/ clusters strongly enough: *question* /kwɛstʃən/. If this is a problem, round your lips as you make the /k/ sound.

STEP 2 FOCUSED PRACTICE

EXERCISE 1: Words with Clusters

A | *Listen and repeat the words.*

1. **sp**eed	6. **gr**ay	11. **fl**ower	16. **qu**estion
2. **st**ay	7. **br**oken	12. **gl**ad	17. **qu**iet
3. **str**anger	8. **thr**ough	13. **fl**at	18. **qu**ick
4. in**st**ead	9. a**fr**aid	14. in**cl**ude	19. lan**gu**age
5. re**sp**ond	10. a**ppr**oach	15. **pr**oblem	20. a**cqu**ainted

B | *PAIRS: Choose two words from each column and say them to your partner.*

EXERCISE 2: Listen for Differences

A | *Listen and repeat the words.*

1. a. parade	**5. a.** Clyde
b. prayed	**b.** collide
2. a. esteem[1]	**6. a.** estrange[3]
b. steam	**b.** strange
3. a. polite	**7. a.** claps
b. plight[2]	**b.** collapse
4. a. state	**8. a.** sport
b. estate	**b.** support

9. a. black
b. back
10. a. grass
b. gas
11. a. please
b. peas
12. a. kite
b. quite

B | *Listen again and circle the words you hear.*

C | *PAIRS: Say a word from Part A. Your partner will tell you which word you said.*

EXERCISE 3: Differences in Meaning

A | *Listen and write the word you hear in the blank.*

1. I'd like the first _____ (floor/four).

2. Did you say "_____" (prayed/parade)?

3. I love the smell of _____ (gas/grass).

4. Put the _____ (flattest/fattest) package on top.

5. Is the _____ (state/estate) in the north?

6. Did you say "_____" (kick/quick)?

7. If you do this right, you'll have a lot of _____ (steam/esteem).

8. The _____ (plants/pants) are new.

B | *PAIRS: Compare your answers. Then choose a sentence from Part A and complete it with one of the words in parentheses. Your partner will tell you which word you said.*

---

[1] esteem: *respect or high opinion for someone;* [2] plight: *a difficult situation;* [3] estrange: *to keep apart or stay away*

EXERCISE 4: Sentences Full of Sounds

A | *Listen and repeat the sentences. Group words together and speak smoothly.*

1. The estate taxes are higher than the state taxes.

2. We prayed the parade would proceed as planned.

3. I scream, you scream, we all scream for ice cream.

4. Answer the quiz questions quickly but quietly, and don't forget to quote the queen.

5. The crowd of clever climbers clad in clean climbing clothes crossed the clearing to the cliff.

B | *PAIRS: Practice the sentences. Take turns.*

STEP 3   COMMUNICATION PRACTICE

BREAKING UP

EXERCISE 5: We Haven't Been Getting Along

A | *Listen to the conversation.*

AIKO: What's up? You look terrible!

ALEX: Anita just broke up with me. She dumped me!

AIKO: That's too bad. But you two were fighting a lot.

ALEX: I know we haven't been getting along. The problem is the way she broke up with me.

AIKO: What do you mean?

ALEX: She used a break-up service. She paid someone to call me and break up with me—because she didn't want to do it herself.

AIKO: That does sound bad . . . but, uh, Alex, do you remember the name of the service? You know John and I haven't been getting along very well . . . .

> ### Natural English
>
> In phrasal verbs like *break up* or *get along*, join the two words in the phrase closely together. Stress the preposition.
>
> She broke úp with me.
>
> We haven't been getting alóng.
>
> When the two words are used as a noun or adjective, stress the first word.
>
> a bréak-up service
>
> a smooth táke-off

B | *PAIRS: Practice the conversation. Take turns.*

EXERCISE 6: Your Turn

A | *How should you break up with someone? Read the suggestions below. Write* **G** *if you think the suggestion is a good one and write* **B** *if you think it's a bad one.*

_____ use a break-up service

_____ tell the person face-to-face

_____ tell the person over the phone

_____ tell the person in an email

_____ ask a friend to tell the person

_____ avoid seeing or talking to the person ever again

B | *GROUPS: Compare your answers. Do you and your classmates agree? What are some other ways to break up with someone?*

STEP 4   EXTENDED PRACTICE

Accuracy Practice *Listen again to Exercises 1A and 2A on pages 123 and 124. Then record the words.*

Fluency Practice *What's the best way to break up with someone? Record your answer to the question.*

Many English words end in consonant clusters.

help test large glimpse

Verb and Noun Endings

Verb and noun endings can create consonant clusters.

dog /g/   dogs /gz/

like /k/   liked /kt/

shark /rk/   sharks /rks/

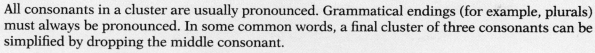

Simplifying Final Clusters

All consonants in a cluster are usually pronounced. Grammatical endings (for example, plurals) must always be pronounced. In some common words, a final cluster of three consonants can be simplified by dropping the middle consonant.

acts   asked   gifts
/æks/   /æst/   /gɪfs/

Joining Final Consonants to the Next Word

1. **Final Consonant + Vowel**

   Join a final consonant to a following vowel clearly.

   hold on leave early park entrance

2. **Final Consonant + Identical Consonant**

   Don't say the consonant twice. Make one long consonant.

   bad day work quickly dress simply

3. **Final Consonant + Different Consonant**

   Pronounce the final consonant, but keep it short (ˀ). Say the next word immediately. Don't separate the consonants with a vowel sound.

   bookˀ bag roseˀ garden sharpˀ knife

EXERCISE 1: Final Consonant Clusters

A | *Listen and repeat the words.*

1. **a.** bell
    b. belt

2. **a.** men
    b. meant

3. **a.** car
    b. card

4. **a.** stress
    b. stressed

5. **a.** hole
    b. hold

6. **a.** fell
    b. felt

7. **a.** were
    b. word

8. **a.** lamb
    b. lamp

B | *Listen again and circle the words you hear.*

C | *PAIRS: Say a word from Part A. Your partner will tell you which word you said.*

EXERCISE 2: Joining Consonants

Listen and repeat the phrases.

Consonant + Vowel	Consonant + Same Consonant	Consonant + Different Consonant
1. correct answer	6. red door	11. junk food
2. expert advice	7. half full	12. walked fast
3. finished early	8. dark clouds	13. health club
4. piles of paper	9. both thumbs	14. change clothes
5. picked it up	10. deep pool	15. bird bath

EXERCISE 3: Conversations

A | *Listen to the sentences in the left column and complete them with the words you hear.*

Sentences

1. Wait just ten minutes. I have to
   _____ _____.

2. I'm looking for a _____
   _____. I want to
   _____ _____.

3. Do you have this _____
   _____ in a size ten?

4. Let's _____ _____.
   Can I throw away these _____
   _____ _____?

5. I had a really _____
   _____ today. How was yours?

6. Do you want to _____
   _____?

7. Did you pick up the tickets at the
   _____ _____?

8. Have you received my application? I sent it a
   _____ _____?

Responses

a. Sure. I don't need them anymore.

b. Why don't you come with me to mine tonight? I'm taking a kickboxing class.

c. Mine wasn't great either. Let's go shopping. I always feel better when I spend money.

d. Sorry. Everything we have is on the rack.

e. Don't worry. What you're wearing looks great.

f. Hold on a moment. No, we haven't gotten it yet.

g. Yes. There's a great movie on channel 5.

h. Yes. The show starts at 8:30, so we'd better leave now.

B | *PAIRS: Make conversations by matching the sentences and responses. Then practice them with a partner. Take turns.*

I NEED A REST

EXERCISE 4: A Bad Day

🎧 **A** | *Listen to the conversation.*

LUKE: Today was terrible! Everything went wrong.

SONIA: What?

LUKE: I said—everything went wrong!

SONIA: What?

LUKE: Well, I lost my keys, I missed my bus, my boss got mad at me, and then—I broke my glasses. I need a rest!

🎧 **B** | *Listen again. In Luke's lines, circle the words with the highest pitch. Draw intonation lines over Sonia's questions to show whether her voice is rising (◡) or falling (◠).*

Natural English

Use rising intonation on a question word when you need a repetition.

A: I found something.

B: What?

A: I said I found something.

Use falling intonation on the question word to show you want information.

A: I found something.

B: What?

A: Your keys.

C | *PAIRS: Practice the conversation in Part A. Take turns.*

EXERCISE 5: I Don't Have the Time

A | *Listen to the rhyme.*

There ONCE was a GUY who was STRESSED.

He KNEW that he NEEDed a REST.

ReLAXing is FINE,

But I DON'T have the TIME.

ToMORrow we're HAving a TEST.

B | *PAIRS: Practice the rhyme. Stress the capitalized words and use the lines to group words. Take turns.*

EXERCISE 6: Coping and Not Coping with Stress

A | *Read the sentences and check (✓) the statements that describe how you cope (or don't cope) with stress.*

_____ **1.** I eat when I get upset.

_____ **2.** I avoid thinking about my problems.

_____ **3.** I get about five hours of sleep a night.

_____ **4.** At least twice a week, I exercise hard enough to make me sweat.

_____ **5.** I take a break when I'm stressed out.

_____ **6.** I don't have much time for myself.

_____ **7.** I have a friend I can talk to about my problems.

_____ **8.** I eat at least one hot meal a day.

B | *PAIRS: Compare your answers. Which statements describe situations that can reduce stress? Increase stress? Explain.*

STEP 4 EXTENDED PRACTICE

Accuracy Practice *Listen again to Exercises 1A and 2 on page 128. Then record the words and phrases.*

Fluency Practice *Record a description of a bad day you had in the past. Use your voice to show how you felt and pay attention to the ends of words. Join words together and speak smoothly and clearly.*

PART III

STRESS IN WORDS

26 Stress in Words: Overview

STEP 1 PRESENTATION

A syllable is a "beat" of a word. The word *visit* has two syllables. The first syllable in *visit* is stressed. The stressed syllable is the most important syllable in the word; listeners use it to identify the word.

Stressed Syllables

One syllable in a word has primary stress (ʹ). The vowel in the stressed syllable is longer and louder than vowels in other syllables. The stressed vowel is often pronounced on a higher pitch (a higher note).

ví·sit   fás·ter   gó·a

Unstressed Syllables

Unstressed vowels are short and unclear. Most vowels in unstressed syllables are pronounced /ə/ or /ɪ/. Any vowel letter can be pronounced /ə/ if it's unstressed.

agó	lísten	diréct	contról	cáreful
/ə/	/ə/	/ə/	/ə/	/ə/

Secondary Stress

Some words have both primary stress and secondary stress (written "ˋ"). The vowel in a syllable with secondary stress is a full vowel, but it is not pronounced on a high pitch (a high note). In compound nouns (noun + noun), the first noun has primary stress and high pitch. The second noun has secondary stress and low pitch.

aír·pòrt   ráil·ròad

Vowel + Vowel Sequences and Syllables

In some words, two vowel letters represent two vowel sounds, pronounced in different syllables. The first vowel usually ends in a /y/ or /w/ sound, for example /iy/, /ay/, or /uw/. The /y/ or /w/ is used to join the two vowels together.

sci^yence   po^wetry   ide^ya

In other words, two vowel letters written together represent one vowel sound.

boat   bread   four   piece

EXERCISE 1: Listen for Stress

A | *Listen and repeat the word pairs. Put a stress mark (ʹ) over the stressed syllable in each word.*

1. **a.** désert **b.** dessert   4. **a.** decent **b.** descent
2. **a.** record (*noun*) **b.** record (*verb*)   5. **a.** really **b.** rely
3. **a.** message **b.** massage   6. **a.** mystic **b.** mistake

B | *Listen and write the words you hear in the blanks.*

1. I had a delicious _____ in the _____. (desert/dessert)

2. They'll _____ the grades in the _____ book. (récord/recórd)

3. Did you say "_____" or "_____"? (really/rely)

4. The spa left a _____ about your _____. (message/massage)

5. The _____ made a _____. (mystic/mistake)

C | *PAIRS: Practice reading the sentences. Check your partner's stress.*

EXERCISE 2: Syllable Patterns

A | *Listen to the words. Tap the syllables with your finger and write the number of syllables in the blank. Then put a stress mark (ʹ) over the stressed syllable.*

1. guitár __2__   5. nutrition ____   9. musical ____
2. medical ____   6. dinner ____   10. total ____
3. parents ____   7. arrangement ____   11. afford ____
4. enjoy ____   8. history ____   12. pollution ____

B | *Write each word under one of the syllable patterns below ("ʹ" means a stressed syllable and "◡" means an unstressed syllable.)*

ʹ◡	◡ʹ	ʹ◡◡	◡ʹ◡
_____	*guitar*	_____	_____
_____	_____	_____	_____
_____	_____	_____	_____

EXERCISE 3: Listen for Syllables

🎧 *Listen and repeat the words. Write **1** if the bold letters are pronounced as one vowel sound. Write **2** if they're pronounced as two vowel sounds, and write the joining sound (**y** or **w**) between the two vowels.*

1. br**ea**k ___1___
2. cre^y**a**te ___2___
3. n**eo**n _____
4. p**eo**ple _____

5. soc**ie**ty _____
6. bel**ie**ve _____
7. qu**ie**t _____
8. s**ui**t _____

9. soc**ia**l _____
10. immed**ia**tely _____
11. z**oo**logy _____
12. z**oo** _____

EXERCISE 4: Listen for Differences

🎧 **A** | *Listen and repeat the compound nouns and adjective-noun phrases.*

Compound Noun

Adjective + Noun

1. Whíte Hòuse
   whíte hóuse

2. yéllow jàcket
   yéllow jácket

3. bláckbòard
   bláck bóard

4. dárkròom
   dárk róom

5. a rédèye[1]
   a réd éye

🎧 **B** | *Listen again and circle the phrases you hear.*

EXERCISE 5: Fill In the Grid

PAIRS: Each of you has a grid that is partially complete. Don't show your grid to your partner. Take turns asking each other for missing words. When you finish, compare your grids. They should be the same. Student A's grid is on page 204. Student B's grid is on page 207.

What's in box A2?

---

[1] a redeye: *an overnight flight*

A LONG LIFE

EXERCISE 6: Life Expectancy

A | *Listen to the conversation.*

MARTA: I'm going to live to be 102 years old!

MIKE: How do you know that? You're only 33 now.

MARTA: I found a life expectancy calculator online. It asks you a lot of questions and then calculates your life expectancy.

MIKE: What were the questions? Like whether you smoke?*

MARTA: Yeah. That was a lifestyle question. There were also questions about your personal life, like how much you work. And there were questions about nutrition and medical history.

---

*Natural English

In informal, spoken English, you can use the word *like* to introduce sentences. The meaning is "for example".

Like whether you smoke?

In formal English, *like* is only a preposition and cannot introduce sentences.

B | *PAIRS: Practice the conversation. Take turns.*

EXERCISE 7: Life Expectancy Factors

A | *Listen to some factors that influence life expectancy. Put a stress mark (ˈ) over the stressed syllable in each underlined word.*

1. your <u>marital</u> <u>status</u>
   (single, married, divorced)

2. your <u>cholesterol</u>[1]

3. your blood pressure[2]

4. your <u>level</u> of <u>education</u>

5. smoking

6. your height and weight

7. <u>regular</u> check ups with a doctor and dentist

8. your weekly <u>alcohol</u> <u>consumption</u> (number of drinks)

9. the number of fruits or <u>vegetables</u> you eat in a day

10. your general <u>attitude</u>[3] (<u>optimistic</u> or <u>pessimistic</u>)

11. the amount of air <u>pollution</u>[4] where you live

12. the number of times a week you eat red meat

B | *PAIRS: How would you categorize the life expectancy factors in Part A? Write each factor on the corresponding line below. Can you think of other factors that might be important to increasing life expectancy? Which factors do you think are the most important?*

Personal/Lifestyle _____

_____

_____

Nutrition _____

_____

_____

Medical _____

_____

_____

STEP 4 EXTENDED PRACTICE

Accuracy Practice *Listen again to Exercises 1B and 2A on page 135. Then record the sentences and words.*

Fluency Practice *What are the advantages and disadvantages to living a long life? Record your answer.*

---

[1] cholesterol: *a substance in your body that may cause heart disease;* [2] blood pressure: *the power with which blood moves through your body;* [3] attitude: *your positive or negative feelings about something;* [4] air pollution: *a state in which the air contains gases or dust in harmful amounts*

UNIT 27 Stressed Syllables; Vowel Length; Vowel Reduction

STEP 1 PRESENTATION

The alternation of stressed and unstressed syllables is a key to natural sounding English. Stressing words correctly helps listeners identify the words you say.

Syllables

A syllable is a "beat" of a word. The center of a syllable is usually a vowel.

cat   doctor   important

1 beat   2 beats   3 beats

Stress

1. Stressed Vowels/Syllables

The stressed syllable is the most important syllable in a word.

Vowels in syllables with primary stress (ˊ) are longer and louder than other vowels. Vowels with primary stress may be pronounced on a high pitch (a high note).

stúdent   to**dáy**   **wón**derful

2. Unstressed Vowels/Syllables

Unstressed vowels are short. They can be spelled with any vowel letter, but are usually pronounced the same: /ə/ or /ɪ/.

| Pronunciation: | chíckən | léssən | əccúr | wómən |
| Spelling: | chick**e**n | less**o**n | **o**ccur | wom**a**n |

3. Secondary Stress

Some words have syllables with secondary stress (ˋ). Vowels with secondary stress are full vowels (not reduced), but they're not pronounced on a high pitch.

aír`pòrt`   róom`màte`

STEP 2 FOCUSED PRACTICE

EXERCISE 1: Stress Patterns

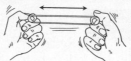

Listen and repeat the words. Make the stressed vowels long. (Pretend you're stretching a rubber band when you say the stressed vowel.) The words in each column have the same stress pattern.

1. **mu**sic
2. **pro**mise
3. **tra**vel
4. **ha**ppen

5. oc**cur**
6. a**fraid**
7. de**cide**
8. to**day**

9. a**no**ther
10. to**mor**row
11. re**mem**ber
12. pro**fes**sor

13. **pre**sident
14. **na**tional
15. **di**fficult
16. **beau**tiful

EXERCISE 2: Hearing Stress Patterns

Listen and repeat the words. Cross out the word with a different stress pattern.

1. together, tomorrow, tobacco, terrific, ~~totally~~
2. pollution, politics, poetry, popular, possible
3. digital, difficult, discussion, distantly, dieting
4. policeman, chocolate, potato, tomato, Alaska
5. dangerous, criminal, accident, important, practical

EXERCISE 3: Listen for Differences

A | Listen to the phrases and tap the syllables with your finger.

A	B
1. start working _____	started working _____
2. a practice test _____	a practical test _____
3. rent an apartment _____	rented an apartment _____
4. answer a question _____	answered a question _____
5. center field _____	Senator Field _____
6. mother's folks _____	mother's focus _____
7. not quite _____	not quiet _____

B | PAIRS: Underline the syllables in each phrase and write the number of syllables in the blank. Then practice saying the phrases.

EXERCISE 4: Unstressed Vowels

A | *The words below have been "respelled" to show how the unstressed vowels are pronounced. Listen and repeat the words. Then write the correct spelling of each word in the blank.*

1. fáshən dəsìgnər

   fashion designer

2. dátə ànələst

3. pílət

4. présədənt

5. pəlícemən

6. mánəgər

7. trávəl àgənt

8. cəreér ədvìsər

9. prəféssər

10. cənsúltənt

11. phýsəkəl thérəpəst

12. phətógrəphər

B | *PAIRS: Compare your answers. Then practice saying the words to each other. Pronounce the unstressed vowels /ə/. (Note: Unstressed vowels spelled with the letters i or e can be pronounced /ə/ or /ɪ/.)*

EXERCISE 5: Grammatical Endings and Syllables

A | *Grammatical endings, such as **-ed** or **-s**, sometimes add a new syllable to a word. Listen to the word pairs. Circle the word if the underlined ending is pronounced as a new syllable.*

1. plant<u>ed</u>, plann<u>ed</u>

2. listen<u>ed</u>, list<u>ed</u>

3. nose<u>s</u>, note<u>s</u>

4. happen<u>ed</u>, hand<u>ed</u>

5. pea<u>s</u>, piece<u>s</u>

6. request<u>ed</u>, requir<u>ed</u>

7. free<u>s</u>, freeze<u>s</u>

8. wash<u>ed</u>, wast<u>ed</u>

9. answer<u>ed</u>, end<u>ed</u>

10. ache<u>s</u>, age<u>s</u>

11. rest<u>ed</u>, dress<u>ed</u>

12. rose<u>s</u>, rope<u>s</u>

B | *Compare your answers. Then practice saying the word pairs.*

JOBS AND PERSONALITY

EXERCISE 6: I'm Not Comfortable with That

A | *Listen to the conversation.*

JOB COUNSELOR:	We have a job opening that we think you might be interested in.
MARCY:	Really? What is it?
COUNSELOR:	It's a sales position with a biotech[1] company. The company produces hospital equipment.
MARCY:	Tell me more about it.
COUNSELOR:	There's a guaranteed salary, but it isn't very high. Most of your income would come from sales commissions.[2]
MARCY:	I'm not comfortable with that.* I need to know how much I'm making each month.

---

*Natural English

Comfortable is usually pronounced /kə́mftərbəl/, as a three-syllable word.

Use the expression *not comfortable with* + a situation or an idea that makes you feel worried or insecure.

I'm not comfortable with the salary.

I'm not comfortable introducing myself to strangers.

B | *PAIRS: Practice the conversation in Part A. Is the biotech sales job a good job for Marcy? Explain. Do you think Marcy is making the right decision? Why or why not?*

---

[1] biotech: *biological technology;* [2] sales commissions: *amounts of money paid to someone for selling something*

EXERCISE 7: Matching Characteristics and Professions

A | *Listen and repeat. Make sure you understand the words and phrases.*

artículate	courágeous	fríendly	íntroverted	lógical
adáptable	creátive	hónest	intúitive	methódical
cómfortable with uncértainty	cúrious	imáginative	obsérvant	pátient
compétitive	decísive	intélligent	óutgoing	sénsitive

B | *What characteristics should a police officer have? A lawyer? A fashion designer? An entrepreneur? Look at the characteristics in the box. Choose three characteristics for each profession and write them on the lines below. Then add another profession and three more characteristics to the list.*

1. Police officer _____

2. Lawyer _____

3. Fashion designer _____

4. Entrepreneur _____

5. _____ _____

C | *PAIRS: Compare your answers. Then choose three characteristics from Part A that describe you and your profession.*

STEP 4 EXTENDED PRACTICE

Accuracy Practice *Listen again to Exercises 1 and 5A on pages 140 and 141. Then record the words.*

Fluency Practice *Record your answers to the questions below. You can use your own words or those in Exercise 7A.*

1. What characteristics should a politician have? Why?
2. Do politicians usually have these characteristics? Explain.

STEP 1 PRESENTATION

The stressed syllable can be predicted in some types of words. Knowing predictable stress patterns will help you pronounce new words correctly.

Stress and Parts of Speech

1. Two-Syllable Nouns and Adjectives

Most two-syllable nouns and adjectives are stressed on the first syllable.

fámous   fáther   húngry   óffice

2. Two-Syllable Verbs

Two-syllable verbs are often stressed on the second syllable. However, some common two-syllable verbs are stressed on the first syllable.

belíeve   invíte   lísten   prómise

Suffixes

Primary stress falls on the syllable before these suffixes: *-tion, -sion, -ic, -ical, -ically, -ity, -ian, -ial, -ialize, -ious, -graphy*.

defíne + tion → definítion   phóto + graphy → photógraphy   fántasy + ic → fantástic

Primary stress falls on these suffixes: *-ese, -eer/-ier, -ee*.

Chína + ese → Chinése   móuntain + eer → mountainéer

Most other suffixes do not change stress in the base word.

góvern + ment → góvernment   predíct + able → predíctable   succéss + ful → succéssful

Numbers

1. Numbers Ending in *-teen*

The *t* in *-teen* has a clear /t/ sound. Stress the last syllable of a *-teen* number when it ends a sentence.

A: How many stamps do you want?   **B:** I need 18 (eightéen).

Stress the first syllable of a *-teen* number in years.

1990 (níneteen nínety)

The first syllable of a *-teen* number is often stressed when the next word begins with a stressed syllable.

18 Main Street (éighteen Máin Stréet)

2. Numbers Ending in *-ty*

The first syllable of *-ty* numbers is always stressed. The letter *t* sounds like a "fast d" (a quickly pronounced /d/ sound).

éighty   síxty

EXERCISE 1: Words with Suffixes

🎧 *The suffixes in the words below determine which syllable receives stress. Listen and repeat the words. Put a stress mark (ʹ) over the stressed syllable.*

1. *-tion/sion*

    a. organization

    b. permission

    c. identification

2. *-ic*

    a. scientific

    b. realistic

    c. fantastic

3. *-eer/ier*

    a. volunteer

    b. engineer

    c. financier

4. *-ity*

    a. publicity

    b. majority

    c. ability

5. *-graphy*

    a. biography

    b. photography

    c. geography

6. *-ial*

    a. editorial

    b. memorial

    c. official

EXERCISE 2: Predicting Stress

🎧 **A |** *Review the rules for suffixes on page 144. Then listen to the words in column A. Put a stress mark (ʹ) over the stressed vowels in column B.*

A	B
1. compéte	competítion, competitive
2. édit	editor, editorial
3. públic	publicity, publicly
4. phótograph	photographic, photographer
5. prófit	profiteer, profitable, profitability
6. círculate	circulatory, circulation
7. óffice	official, officer

B | *PAIRS: Practice the words. Take turns.*

EXERCISE 3: Conversations

PAIRS: Complete the conversations with the correct form of the word in parentheses. Put a stress mark (ˊ) over the stressed syllable. Then practice the conversations.

1. (photograph)

   A: That's a beautiful _____*phótograph*_____! Who took it?

   B: Tim. He's a professional _____.

   A: Did he go to school for that?

   B: No. I guess he's a natural. He's never taken a _____ class.

2. (edit)

   A: Guess what? I've been chosen as the _____ of the school newspaper

   next year!

   B: Does that mean you have to _____ all the articles? That doesn't sound good.

   A: Oh—I hope not. I'm hoping it means I get to write the _____.

3. (compete)

   A: My roommate is so _____!

   B: What do you mean? Who does she _____ with?

   A: Me. All of her classmates. Every course she takes is a _____, and she always

   has to win.

EXERCISE 4: Listen for Differences: -*ate* endings

A | *When the suffix -**ate** is a verb ending, it's pronounced /eyt/ (like "ate"). When the suffix is a noun or adjective ending, it's unstressed and pronounced /ət/. Listen and repeat the words.*

Verbs:	duplicate	graduate	separate
Nouns/adjectives:	duplicate	graduate	separate

B | PAIRS: Complete each sentence with the word in parentheses. Write **(V)** if the word is a verb and the suffix is pronounced /eyt/. Write **(N)** if the word is a noun or adjective and the suffix is pronounced /ət/. Then practice the sentences. Take turns.

1. (duplicate)

   I don't know whether he wants the original or a ____*duplicate (N)*____.

   If he wants a _____, I'll have to _____ the original.

2. (graduate)

   When you _____ from college, are you going to apply to

   _____ school?

3. (separate)

   Recycling Rules: Please _____ the bottles from the cans and

   put them in _____ containers.

EXERCISE 5: Listen for Differences

A | Listen and repeat the numbers.

1. 13 (thirteen)	6. 18 (eighteen)	11. 60 (sixty)
2. 14 (fourteen)	7. 19 (nineteen)	12. 70 (seventy)
3. 15 (fifteen)	8. 30 (thirty)	13. 80 (eighty)
4. 16 (sixteen)	9. 40 (forty)	14. 90 (ninety)
5. 17 (seventeen)	10. 50 (fifty)	

B | Listen to the conversations. Complete the sentences with the numbers you hear.

1. **A:** My brother is going to be _____ tomorrow.

   B: _____?! I didn't know you had a brother that old!

   A: Old? _____ is old?

   B: Did you say "forty" or "fourteen"?

   A: _____.

2. **A:** The next train to Boston leaves at _____.

   B: I'm sorry—did you say _____ or _____?

   A: _____.

(continued on next page)

3. A: My address is _____ First Avenue.

   B: _____ First Avenue?

   A: No. _____.

   B: OK. _____ First Avenue. My mother lives at _____

   First Avenue. That's not far from you.

C | *PAIRS: Compare your answers. Then practice the conversations. Choose different numbers in Part A and use them to make new conversations.*

WHAT DO YOU KNOW ABOUT HISTORY?

EXERCISE 6: History in the *-teens* and *-tys*

PAIRS: You and your partner each have four dates with and without historical events. All of the dates end in -teen or -ty numbers. Don't show your dates or events to your partner. Take turns choosing a date and asking your partner what happened on that date. Pronounce the date clearly. Your partner will tell you what happened. Student A's information is on page 204. Student B's information is on page 207.

EXAMPLE:

STUDENT A: What happened in <u>1950</u>?

STUDENT B: <u>*Indonesia became independent.*</u>

EXERCISE 7: Don't Know Much about History

A | *Listen to the paragraph. Put a stress mark (ˈ) over the most heavily stressed word in the underlined phrases.*

Jay Leno is the host of "The Tonight Show," a late-night <u>talk show</u> produced in California. In some shows, he has a popular segment called "Jaywalking." Leno and a <u>camera crew</u> go out on the streets of Los Angeles and interview ordinary people. Leno asks people easy questions about <u>well-known</u> topics from history, geography, or current events. The interviews are funny because the people don't know the answers. A sample interview might sound like the following:

LENO:	In what country can you find the Panama Canal?
INTERVIEWEE:	Uh . . . I don't know.
LENO:	OK. Let's try another question. In what country can you find the Great Wall of China?
INTERVIEWEE:	I know the answer to that one. China.
LENO:	OK. Let's try the first question again. In what country can you find the Panama Canal?
INTERVIEWEE:	Uh . . . China?

Natural English

The underlined phrases are compound adjectives. Stress compound adjectives like compound nouns: The first word is stressed more heavily than the second. Compound adjectives are often written with a hyphen (-).

láte-nìght talk show

wéll-knòwn topics from history

a fíve-mìnute break

B | *PAIRS: Practice the interview in Part A. Then make your own interview. Change **Panama Canal** to another place name. Take turns.*

EXERCISE 8: Making History Interesting

The Jaywalking interviews may not be evidence that Americans don't know enough about history. People in the interviews might give funny, wrong answers on purpose because they want to be on TV. Still, educators believe that the emphasis on math and science in high school tests probably means that history classes aren't as important to students. They believe history classes would be more interesting if they showed students how past events are relevant to the present and future.

GROUPS: Answer the questions.

1. When you were in high school, did you like history? Explain.

2. How important is knowing history?

STEP 4 EXTENDED PRACTICE

Accuracy Practice *Listen again to Exercises 1 and 5A on pages 145 and 147. Then record the words and numbers.*

Fluency Practice *Record your answers to the questions in Exercise 8.*

STEP 1 PRESENTATION

Many nouns are stressed on the first syllable. Compound nouns follow this pattern, with stress on the first word. Words like *record*, which can be nouns or verbs, have two stress patterns. They're stressed on the first syllable as nouns and on the last syllable as verbs.

Compound Nouns

Compound nouns are two nouns used together as one noun. Pronounce the first noun with heavy stress and high pitch. Pronounce the second noun with secondary stress and low pitch.

póst⎤   raíl⎤   schóol⎤
     ⎿ òffice   ⎿ ròad   ⎿ bùs

1. **Spelling**

    Some compound nouns are written as one word; others are written as two words.

    database   password

    identity thief   bike path

2. **Phrasal Verbs Used as Nouns**

    Use the stress-pitch pattern of compound nouns.

          máke⎤   táke⎤
    I bought some new   ⎿ùp.   The   ⎿òff has been delayed by an hour.

Noun-Verb Pairs

Some two-syllable words are nouns when stress is on the first syllable. They become verbs when stress is on the second syllable.

Noun: a présent   a récord

Verb: to presént   to record

EXERCISE 1: Compound Nouns

🎧 *Listen and repeat the words.*

1.	birth date	8.	greenhouse
2.	graduate school	9.	footbridge
3.	White House	10.	orange juice
4.	age limit	11.	driver's license
5.	travel agent	12.	darkroom
6.	employment history	13.	report card
7.	fingerprints	14.	blood type

EXERCISE 2: Listen for Differences: Stress patterns

🎧 *Listen to the phrases. Circle the phrase that has the compound stress-pitch pattern (heavy stress and high pitch on the first word and secondary stress and low pitch on the second word).*

	A	B
1.	a blackboard	a black board
2.	the post office	the new office
3.	paper napkins	paper clips
4.	a birthday card	a beautiful card
5.	an impressive building	an office building
6.	fresh juice	grape juice
7.	a lighthouse[1]	a light color
8.	a greenhouse[2]	a green house
9.	my good friend	my boyfriend
10.	rock music	popular music

---

[1] lighthouse: *a tower with a bright light that guides ships away from danger near land;* [2] greenhouse: *a glass structure for growing plants*

EXERCISE 3: Conversations

A | *Listen and complete the sentences in the left column with the words you hear.*

Sentences

_h_ **1.** Please enter your _____.

____ **2.** Somebody left a _____ in

class yesterday.

____ **3.** Did you go to the _____?

____ **4.** What's the _____?

____ **5.** Did you visit the _____?

____ **6.** I got my _____!

____ **7.** What's the _____ for

tomorrow?

____ **8.** What time do you have to leave for

the _____?

Responses

a. Yes. I bought some vitamins.

b. Eighteen years old.

c. Yes, but I didn't see the president.

d. My flight leaves at 8:00, so probably 5:30.

e. Congratulations! I guess you finally learned to park.

f. It's mine. I wondered what happened to it.

g. Heavy rain and high winds.

h. I didn't know I had one. I don't remember it.

B | *PAIRS: Make conversations by matching the sentences and responses. Then practice them with a partner. Take turns.*

EXERCISE 4: Listen for Differences: Noun-verb pairs

A | *Listen and repeat the words.*

	Noun	Verb			Noun	Verb
1.	**a.** cónvert	**b.** convért	**5.**	**a.** pérmit	**b.** permít
2.	**a.** récord	**b.** recórd	**6.**	**a.** cónvict	**b.** convíct
3.	**a.** rébel	**b.** rebél	**7.**	**a.** óbject	**b.** objéct
4.	**a.** súspect	**b.** suspéct	**8.**	**a.** prótest	**b.** protést

B | *Listen again and circle the words you hear.*

C | *Choose a word from Part A and say it to the class. Your classmates will tell you whether you said a noun or a verb.*

KEEPING PERSONAL INFORMATION PRIVATE

EXERCISE 5: Passwords

A | *Listen to the conversation.*

CUSTOMER SERVICE:	How can I help you, Mr. Choi?
PATRICK:	I need some information about my account balance. I think there's been a mistake.
CUSTOMER SERVICE:	I'll be happy to help you. Can you type in your password?
PATRICK:	Password? Did I set one up?
CUSTOMER SERVICE:	Yes, you did.
PATRICK:	Can you give me a hint?
CUSTOMER SERVICE:	What was the name of your first pet?
PATRICK:	Oh, OK. Thanks.

Natural English

In questions, *can* has a short, reduced pronunciation: /kən/. *Can* joins closely to surrounding words.

   Howkən I help you? (How can I help you?)

   kənyou give me a hint? (Can you give me a hint?)

B | *PAIRS: Practice the conversation in Part A. Take turns.*

---

¹ account balance: *the amount of money you have in your bank account*

EXERCISE 6: Your Turn

GROUPS: Discuss the questions.

1. Do you have trouble remembering passwords?
2. How careful are you about keeping your personal information private?
3. What kinds of personal information do you provide about yourself in online profiles? Do you think it's safe to share this information with others? Have you ever had a problem sharing this information?

STEP 4   EXTENDED PRACTICE

Accuracy Practice *Listen again to Exercises 1 and 2 on page 152. Then record the words and phrases.*

Fluency Practice *Record your answers to the questions. Concentrate on using correct stress patterns.*

1. When you applied to this school, what personal information did you have to include in the application?
2. If you're a full-time international student, what kinds of personal information did you have to supply to get a visa?

PART

IV

RHYTHM AND INTONATION

Rhythm and Intonation: Overview

STEP 1 PRESENTATION

Rhythm is the pattern of strong and weak (stressed and unstressed) syllables in phrases and sentences. Intonation is the pattern of high and low notes. Both rhythm and intonation add meaning.

Rhythm

In English, long, clear syllables alternate with short, less clear syllables. The picture of the skyline illustrates a typical rhythm pattern in English. The big buildings represent the strong syllables; the smaller buildings represent the unstressed syllables.

1. **Content Words and Function Words**

   Rhythm patterns in sentences are like stress patterns in words. In sentences, there are stressed and unstressed words; in words there are stressed and unstressed syllables.

   Content Words: Content words include nouns, verbs, adjectives, and adverbs. Content words have clear meaning and are usually stressed.

   > Jóe's láte.

   Function Words: Function words include articles, prepositions, auxiliary verbs, pronouns, and conjunctions. They're usually unstressed.

   > We can dríve to the béach.

2. **Reduced Words**

   Some function words have reduced pronunciations. The vowels in these words are pronounced /ə/, and consonants may be dropped. Reduced words join closely to surrounding words in the sentence. If you're familiar with these reductions, you'll understand spoken English more easily. Listen as your teacher reads the sentences below.

   > Some are home. (sounds like "summer home")

   > The season will change. (sounds like "The seasonal change.")

3. **Thought Groups**

   The words in a sentence are pronounced in shorter, meaningful phrases, or thought groups. Thought groups help the listener understand the meaningful units within a longer sentence. A thought group has at least one stressed word in it. The words in a thought group are pronounced together smoothly.

   > at hóme   wátch it   the wédding

The number of words you include in a thought group depends partly on meaning and partly on the number of words you can pronounce together smoothly. When you're learning English, you should use shorter thought groups. Look at two ways to group the words in this sentence:

I'm leaving at 10 this evening.   I'm leaving at 10 this evening.

4. **Highlighting Important Words**

In most sentences, one or two words express the most important information. Highlight (emphasize) these words by pronouncing them with strong stress, on a high pitch (a high note).

I'm HUN gry.   She's my MO ther.

Intonation Patterns and Meanings

Intonation is the melody of speech, the pattern of high and low notes. Intonation adds meaning to sentences. For example, when intonation rises at the end of the sentence, it often means the speaker is uncertain. *Yes/No* questions usually end in rising intonation.

Did you like the movie?

Falling intonation can mean that the speaker is certain. Statements often end in falling intonation.

I liked the movie a lot.

STEP 2 FOCUSED PRACTICE

EXERCISE 1: Rhymes

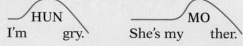 **A** | *In rhymes and poetry, rhythm patterns repeat and are easy to hear. Listen to the rhyme. Stressed words are in capital letters.*

Las VEgas vaCAtions are FUN,

The LIGHTS and the SHOWS and the SUN.

I met MAX the first NIGHT,

It was LOVE at first SIGHT,

I SAID right aWAY, "He's the ONE."

B | *PAIRS: Practice the rhyme. Take turns.*

EXERCISE 2: Conversation

A | *Regular, repeated rhythm patterns sometimes occur in speaking. Listen to the conversation. (ˊ) means a strong/stressed syllable.*

> **A:** The sófa lóoks a líttle táttered.[1]
>
> **B:** We cán't affórd to búy a néw one.
>
> **A:** I knów a pláce that sélls at díscount.
>
> **B:** You méan the pláce that sóld us thís one?

B | *PAIRS: Practice the conversation. Take turns.*

EXERCISE 3: Hearing Rhythm

A | *Listen and repeat the conversation. Put a stress mark (ˊ) over stressed syllables.*

> **A:** I tóld you to thrów it.
>
> **B:** I thought you said kick it.
>
> **A:** We're not playing soccer.
>
> **B:** Well, I didn't know that!

B | *PAIRS: Practice the conversation. Take turns.*

EXERCISE 4: Reduced Words

Listen to the sentences and notice how the function words sound. The underlined words in the sentences have the same (or nearly the same) pronunciation.

1. The <u>baker's</u> going to <u>bake her</u> a special cake.
2. The first <u>reader</u> can't <u>read or</u> write another language.
3. <u>Did he</u> call Mr. <u>Diddy</u>?
4. In the tropics, <u>seas and</u> lakes don't freeze in any <u>season</u>.
5. How much do you need <u>to borrow</u> <u>tomorrow</u>?
6. If the coffee's too strong, <u>we can</u> <u>weaken</u> it.

EXERCISE 5: Minimal Conversation

A | *Listen and repeat the conversation.*

> **LIZ:** Tired?
>
> **MARKO:** Yeah.
>
> **LIZ:** Why?
>
> **MARKO:** Work.

B | *PAIRS: Practice the conversation. Follow the intonation lines.*

---

[1] tattered: *old and torn*

LUCY AND MAX GOT MARRIED

EXERCISE 6: Las Vegas Weddings

A | *Listen and repeat. Make sure you understand the words.*

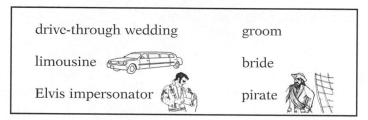

drive-through wedding	groom
limousine	bride
Elvis impersonator	pirate

B | *Listen to the recording and then answer the questions.*

1. Why is Las Vegas known as the "Marriage Capital of the World"?
2. Describe some of the nontraditional weddings available in Las Vegas.
3. Have you ever been to Las Vegas? Would you ever like to go?

EXERCISE 7: Trouble in Los Angeles

Lucy and Max are newlyweds. A month ago, Lucy went to Las Vegas for vacation. She met Max, fell in love, and got married. They're now living in Lucy's apartment in Los Angeles. Max doesn't have a job, and he wants to be an actor.

Natural English

Use the preposition *to* after *get/be married*; don't use *with*.

Lucy got married to Max.

She's married to Max.

Don't use a preposition when *marry* is the verb.

Lucy married Max.

A | *First listen to the phrases in each column and repeat them. Pronounce the words in each phrase as a group.*

A	B	C
The phone company The A1 Modeling Agency Lucy's father	doesn't have any work is very upset wants Lucy to call	about her marriage. for Max. as soon as possible.

B | *Now listen to the recording.*

C | *PAIRS: Match phrases from the three columns in Part A to make sentences that summarize Lucy's messages. Practice the sentences, grouping words into phrases. Then talk about the problems Lucy and Max are having.*

STEP 4   EXTENDED PRACTICE

Accuracy Practice   *Listen again to Exercises 1A and 4 on pages 159 and 160. Then record the rhyme and sentences.*

Fluency Practice   *Record a description of a traditional wedding in your country.*

STEP 1   PRESENTATION

Sentences are made up of strong (stressed) and weak (unstressed) words. Words within sentences are pronounced together in meaningful phrases (thought groups).

Content and Function Words

1. **Strong Words or Content Words**

   Content words have clear meanings. They include nouns, verbs, adjectives, adverbs, question words, and demonstratives (*this/that/these/those*). These words are usually stressed in a sentence.

   > I'm READY to ORDER.

2. **Weak Words or Function Words**

   Function words have grammatical meanings. They include pronouns, prepositions, auxiliary verbs, conjunctions, and articles. These words are usually unstressed. They're shorter and pronounced less clearly than content words. Notice the circled function words in the sentence below.

   > (We) (can) COME (at) NOON.

Thought Groups

Thought groups help the listener organize the meaning of a sentence. They help the speaker by breaking the sentences into shorter parts. Pronounce words in a thought group together, smoothly.

> Some of us are going to leave at 9:00.

1. **Joining Thought Groups**

   When you join thought groups together, pause or lengthen the end of a thought group briefly before starting the next group. There may be a small rise in pitch at the end of a thought group.

   > My flight is arriving at nine o'clock.   I'll call from the airport.
   >
   >   lengthen   lengthen   lengthen

2. **Grammatical Phrases and Thought Groups**

   Grammatical phrases are often thought groups.

Prepositional phrases:	to the airport	at 10	in the morning
Verb + pronoun:	bring it	take them	call her
Short clauses:	If you leave, call me.		

EXERCISE 1: Rhythm

A | *Listen to the conversation. Put a stress mark (ʹ) over stressed syllables. Then underline thought groups.*

CUSTOMER: I'm ready to order.

WAITER: The chicken is yummy.

CUSTOMER: I think I'll have waffles.

WAITER: The waffles are awful!

B | *PAIRS: Practice the conversation. What do you notice about the rhythm pattern?*

EXERCISE 2: Conversations

A | *Listen to the first three lines of each conversation.*

1. **A:** What's the matter?

   B: Marty's sicker.

   A: Call the doctor.

   B: What's her _____?

2. **A:** I need your help to fix the car.

   B: I'll come tonight at ten o'clock.

   A: You said before you'd come at nine.

   B: I'm busy then. I'll come _____.

B | *PAIRS: Complete the last line of each conversation. Choose a word (or words) so the last line has the same rhythm pattern (the same pattern of stressed and unstressed syllables) as the lines before. Then practice the conversations.*

EXERCISE 3: Differences in Meaning

A | *Listen to the conversations. Group words together so the conversations make sense.*

1. **a.** **MARC:** Did you see Tom?

    ALAN: No, I didn't see Tom.

    b. **MARC:** Did you see, Tom?

    TOM: No, I didn't see anything.

2. **a.** **MARC:** Today at nine we're going to meet José.

    MARIA: I've already met José.

    b. **MARC:** Today at nine we're going to meet, José.

    JOSÉ: Sorry. I can't meet at nine.

3. **a.** **MARC:** There are two, year-old children here.

    MARIA: They're my sister's twins.

    b. **MARC:** There are two-year-old children here.

    MARIA: How many?

4. **a.** **MARC:** I can't remember Alicia.

    MARIA: You met Alicia last year.

    b. **MARC:** I can't remember, Alicia.

    ALICIA: You always forget.

5. **a.** **MARC:** I made three, minute-long calls.

    MAX: A minute isn't very long to talk.

    b. **MARC:** I made three-minute-long calls.

    MAX: How many?

6. **a.** **MARY:** I think you know Milan.

    ALICIA: Yes, I know Milan.

    b. **MARY:** I think you know, Milan.

    MILAN: Yes, I've known for a long time.

B | *PAIRS: Practice the conversations. When you say the first line of each conversation, group words together correctly so your partner knows how to respond.*

CHOOSING A JOB

EXERCISE 4: Who's Hiring Historians?

🎧 **A** | *Listen and repeat the sentences. Use the lines to help you group words.*

1. My major in college was African history.

2. My parents said history wasn't a practical major—they wanted me to be a lawyer.

3. "Who's hiring historians?" they said.

4. But they were wrong.

5. I work for the government, in the State Department.[1]

6. My work helps the government make decisions about foreign aid[2] projects.

7. My salary is above average, and the benefits are very good.

8. Compared to my roommate, I don't feel much stress at work.

Natural English

The prepositions *for* and *at* are often pronounced with reduced vowels. When you speak, make sure you don't stress these prepositions.

I work /fər/ the government.

I don't feel much stress /ət/ work.

B | *PAIRS: Say the sentences in Part A. Take turns.*

---

[1] State Department: *a part of the government that is in charge of foreign affairs;* [2] foreign aid: *monetary help given to other countries*

EXERCISE 5: Your Turn

When employment professionals rate careers, they look at several factors: Salary, benefits, workplace safety, and hiring outlook.[1]

A | *Complete the chart below. Write the name of the job you now have or the job you want to get. Then rate the four factors of that job from good (1) to poor (3).*

Name of Job	Salary	Benefits	Workplace Safety	Hiring Outlook

B | *GROUPS: Tell your classmates about the job you described in the chart. Use thought groups when you describe the factors.*

STEP 4 EXTENDED PRACTICE

Accuracy Practice *Listen again to Exercise 3A on page 165. Then record the conversations.*

Fluency Practice *Record a description of the job you have now or one that you want. What do you think about the salary, benefits, workplace safety, and hiring outlook of that job? In your opinion, which factors have the most influence on job satisfaction?*

---

[1] hiring outlook: *the number of jobs available in that profession and the number of jobs expected in the future*

Highlighting Important Words

STEP 1 PRESENTATION

Words that express important information are highlighted by pronouncing them with heavy stress. In addition, they often also have high pitch (a high note). When listeners understand which information is important, they'll understand you better.

Highlight New Information

The last content word of a sentence often presents new information and is highlighted.

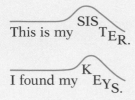

This is my SISTER.

I found my KEYS.

Highlight Contrasting Information

Highlight words that contrast information or correct information.

Hi Sammy!

My name isn't SAMMY—it's SANDY.

Function Words

Function words are usually unstressed in a sentence. You can highlight them if you want to emphasize their meaning.

A: Do you want soup or salad?
B: I want soup AND salad.

STEP 2 FOCUSED PRACTICE

EXERCISE 1: Highlighting Important Words

A | *Listen and repeat the conversations. Circle the highlighted words.*

1. **A:** I'm hungry. What's for dinner?

   B: Nothing. Let's go out.

2. **A:** My pictures were supposed to be ready today.

   B: I didn't tell you that.

3. **A:** It's hot in here.

   B: Open the window.

4. **A:** That's my money you picked up.

   B: No, it's mine. I dropped it.

B | *PAIRS: Practice the conversations. Highlight the important words with heavy stress and high pitch.*

EXERCISE 2: Listen for Differences

A | *Listen and repeat the responses in the right column. Then circle the highlighted words.*

Questions	Responses
1. What did you lose?	**a.** I lost my keys yesterday.
When did you lose your keys?	**b.** I lost my keys yesterday.
Did you find your keys yesterday?	**c.** I lost my keys yesterday.
2. What kind of food don't you like?	**a.** I don't like French food.
You like French food?	**b.** I don't like French food.
You don't like French movies?	**c.** I don't like French food.
3. Who are you going with?	**a.** I'm going to a movie with Joe tonight.
Are you going to a concert with Joe?	**b.** I'm going to a movie with Joe tonight.
You're going to a movie with Joe next week?	**c.** I'm going to a movie with Joe tonight.

B | *PAIRS: Compare your answers. Then make conversations by matching the questions and responses. Highlight the important words.*

EXAMPLE:

STUDENT A: What did you lose?

STUDENT B: I lost my <u>KEYS</u> yesterday.

EXERCISE 3: Highlight Corrections

A | *Listen to the conversation.*

CHAIRMAN:	We have some CHANGES to announce about the neighborhood PARTY. We've moved it from THURSDAY night to FRIDAY night.
COMMITTEE MEMBER:	Um . . . I think we decided SATURDAY.
CHAIRMAN:	Oh, RIGHT. SATURDAY. It's going to start at NINE, NOT eight.
COMMITTEE MEMBER:	I THINK we decided eight-THIRTY.
CHAIRMAN:	Oh yes, yes. And ONE last change. The party's going to be at the CoMMUnity Center, NOT the PLAYground.
COMMITTEE MEMBER:	Uh, no. We DIDN'T change the place. It's STILL at the PLAYground.

B | *PAIRS: Practice the conversation. Use high pitch and heavy stress to highlight the words in capital letters. Take turns.*

EXERCISE 4: Correct Me If I'm Wrong

A | *Read the sentences. The underlined word in each sentence is factually incorrect. Write the correct information in the blanks. (You can check your answers on page 172.)*

Russia	**1.** Canada is the largest country in the world in area.
_____	**2.** Peru is the largest country in South America.
_____	**3.** Montana is the largest state in the United States in area.
_____	**4.** The Amazon River is the longest river in the world.
_____	**5.** The Hudson River is the longest river in the United States.
_____	**6.** The elephant is the largest mammal in the world.
_____	**7.** The buffalo is the largest land mammal in the world.
_____	**8.** India is the most populous country in the world.
_____	**9.** New York is the most populous state in the United States.

B | *GROUPS: Read a sentence aloud. A classmate will correct your sentence using stress and high pitch to highlight the correction.*

EXAMPLE:

STUDENT A: Canada is the largest country in the world in area.

STUDENT B: No. RUSSIA is the largest.

NEIGHBORS

EXERCISE 5: Can You Help Me?

A | *Listen and repeat the conversation. The highlighted words are in bold.*

FELIX: Sorry to **bother** you. I'm **Felix**, your **neighbor** across the **hall**.

NEIGHBOR: Uh-huh.

FELIX: Uh* . . . I was **wondering** if you could help me **out**. Uh . . . are you going to be here tomorrow **afternoon**?

NEIGHBOR: I'm not **sure**. **Why** do you want to **know**?

FELIX: Well, my **cousin** is coming from **Texas** tomorrow afternoon. I can't be here to let her **in**, and I was **wondering** if I could give you my **keys**. She could ring your **bell** and get the **keys**.

---

*Natural English

The hesitation word in English is *uh* (/ə/). It is usually pronounced with a level pitch (note).

Uh . . . I was wondering if you could help me out.

Uh . . . Are you going to be here tomorrow afternoon?

B | *PAIRS: Practice the conversation.*

C | *PAIRS: Answer the questions about the conversation in Part A.*

1. How well does Felix know his neighbor?
2. Do you think Felix's neighbor will agree to take the keys?
3. Would you give your neighbor your keys? Would you take the keys from Felix? Explain.

EXERCISE 6: Your Turn

A | *Ask two classmates the questions in the chart and write their answers in the correct columns.*

Questions	Student's Name: _____	Student's Name: _____
Do you know your neighbors' names?		
Do you greet your neighbors when you see them?		
Do you spend time with your neighbors?		
Can you ask your neighbors for favors?[1]		
Would you do favors for your neighbors?		

B | *Choose one of the questions from the chart and compare your classmates' answers. Use high pitch and heavy stress to highlight contrasts and comparisons.*

EXAMPLES:

ROBERTO knows ONE of his neighbors. SYLVIA doesn't know ANY.

ROBERTO greets his neighbors when he sees them. SO does SYLVIA.

ROBERTO wouldn't ask his neighbors for a favor. NEITHER would SYLVIA.

STEP 4   EXTENDED PRACTICE

Accuracy Practice *Listen again to Exercise 1A on page 169. Then record the conversations.*

Fluency Practice *What are the advantages and disadvantages of knowing your neighbors? Record your answers.*

---

[1] favor: *something you do for someone to help or be kind to him/her*

EXERCISE 4A: 1. Russia, 2. Brazil, 3. Alaska, 4. the Nile River, 5. the Mississippi River, 6. the whale, 7. the elephant, 8. China, 9. California

Reduced Words

STEP 1 PRESENTATION

The function words *and*, *or*, and *can* have reduced pronunciations. The reduced pronunciations are standard English, not slang. You'll understand English better if you're familiar with how these reduced words sound.

And

And is pronounced /ən/. It sounds like the ending of *given* and joins to the preceding word. (Sometimes *and* is written *'n* to show its reduced pronunciation.)

bácon and éggs   bréad and bútter   páper and péncil

Or

Or is pronounced /ər/, like the *-er* ending of *bigger*. *Or* joins to the preceding word.

sóup or sálad   ríght or wróng   ráin or snów

Can

1. *Can* is pronounced /kən/ or /kn/ inside a sentence. It's unstressed and sounds like the last syllable of *chicken*. Join *can* closely to the surrounding words in a sentence. If you stress *can* or pronounce it with the vowel /æ/, your listener may think you've said *can't*.

   May can cook chicken.   Cho can play the piano.
      /kən/   /kən/

2. Stress *can* in short answers or when it's not followed by a verb. Use the full vowel /æ/.

   Yes, I cán.   If I cán, I'll go.
     /kæn/   /kæn/

Can't

Can't is stressed and pronounced /kænt/, with a full vowel.

I cán't do this homework.   We cán't go.
 /kænt/   /kænt/

EXERCISE 1: Phrases with *and* and *or*

🎧 *The single word and the underlined words have the same pronunciation. Listen and repeat.*

1. redden   <u>red and</u> white
2. often[1]   <u>off and</u> on
3. given   <u>give and</u> take
4. eaten   <u>eat and</u> drink

5. runner   <u>run or</u> walk
6. worker   <u>work or</u> play
7. buyer   <u>buy or</u> sell
8. cleaner   <u>clean or</u> dirty

EXERCISE 2: Listen for Differences: *and* vs. *or*

🎧 *Listen to the phrases and fill in the blanks with* **and** *or* **or**.

1. red _____ white
2. red _____ black
3. come _____ go

4. lunch _____ dinner
5. mother _____ father
6. land _____ sea

EXERCISE 3: Sentences with *Can*

🎧 *The single word and the underlined words have the same or almost the same pronunciation. Listen and repeat.*

1. weaken   <u>We can</u> go.
2. awaken   <u>A way can</u> be found.
3. bacon   Mr. <u>Bay can</u> come.

4. beacon   <u>Bea can</u> speak French.
5. shaken   <u>Shay can</u> cook bacon.
6. token   My <u>toe can</u> bend.

EXERCISE 4: Listen for Differences: *can* vs. *can't*

🎧 *Listen to the sentences and fill in the blanks with* **can** *or* **can't**.

1. She _____ swim.
2. Juan _____ drive.
3. Don't call me if you _____ come.

4. Call me if you _____ come.
5. I _____ go this weekend.
6. I _____ bring it to you later.

---

[1] *Most Americans do not pronounce the* t *in* often: of*t*en.

EXERCISE 5: Sounds Like . . .

A | Homophrases *are two phrases that sound the same (or nearly the same) but have different meanings and spellings. Listen to the phrases.*

1. a chicken egg   <u>a chick and egg</u>

2. blacker gray   _____

3. soak an eye   _____

4. the former meaning   _____

5. a customer habit   _____

B | *PAIRS: Think of another phrase with* **and, or,** *or* **can** *that sounds the same (or nearly the same) and write it in the blank. (You can check your answers on page 177.) Then practice saying the homophrases.*

STEP 3   COMMUNICATION PRACTICE

SKILLS

EXERCISE 6: Are You the Right Person for the Job?

A | *Listen and repeat the conversations.*

1. **JOB COUNSELOR:** This company is looking for someone who can speak Chinese.

   JOB SEEKER:[1] I can do that. I'm fluent in Chinese.

   JOB COUNSELOR: Great!

2. **JOB COUNSELOR:** This company is looking for someone who can travel.

   JOB SEEKER: I can't do that. I have young children.

   JOB COUNSELOR: OK. We'll have to keep looking.

> **Natural English**
>
> When *can* follows a pronoun, stress the pronoun more strongly.
>
>   Í can do that.
>
> When *can't* follows a pronoun, stress *can't* more strongly.
>
>   I cán't do that.

---

[1] Job seeker: *someone who's looking for a job*

B | *PAIRS: Make short conversations with your partner. Use the conversations in Part A as examples.*

STUDENT A: Start as a job counselor. Using the information on page 204, tell your partner what skills an employee in your company requires. If your partner says, "I can do that," answer, "Great!" If your partner says, "I can't do that," answer, "OK. We'll have to keep looking." Then switch roles.

STUDENT B: Start as a job seeker. When your partner tells you what skills the company requires, answer, "I can do that" or "I can't do that." Pronounce *can* or *can't* carefully. Then switch roles. Your information is on page 208.

EXERCISE 7: Your Turn

A | *Read the skills in the chart. Check (✓) the skills you have. Then use the blank at the bottom of each section to add other skills.*

Skills	You	Your Partner
Practical life skills		
drive	_____	_____
manage my time	_____	_____
cook	_____	_____
live within my means[1]	_____	_____
_____	_____	_____
Athletic skills		
swim	_____	_____
ride a horse	_____	_____
sail a boat	_____	_____
dunk a basketball	_____	_____
_____	_____	_____
Musical/Artistic skills		
play an instrument (piano/guitar/drums, etc.)	_____	_____
dance (ballet/ballroom/salsa, etc.)	_____	_____
draw/paint landscapes	_____	_____
sing	_____	_____
_____	_____	_____

---

[1] live within my means: *not spend more money than I have*

176   UNIT 33

B | PAIRS: Use **can** or **can't** to tell your partner about your skills. Pronounce **can** or **can't** carefully. Your partner will check (✓) the skills you have in his or her chart. Then switch roles.

STEP 4 EXTENDED PRACTICE

🎧🎤 **Accuracy Practice** Listen again to Exercises 1 and 3 on page 174. Then record the words, phrases, and sentences.

🎤 **Fluency Practice** Record six sentences. In three of the sentences, name two skills you have, joined with **and**. In the other three sentences, name two skills you don't have, joined with **or**. Pronounce **can** and **can't** carefully. Follow the examples.

EXAMPLES:

Í can speak English and Chinese.
 /kən/

I cán't drive or change a tire.

STEP 1 PRESENTATION

Auxiliary verbs such as *am*, *is*, *are*, and *have* are usually unstressed.

Contractions

Use contractions after pronouns. Contractions will make your English sound more natural and "friendlier."

am/is/are	*have/has/had*	*would*
I'm a student.	**I've** already seen that.	**I'd** like French fries.
She's an artist.	**She's** lived here since May.	**She'd** rather drive.
You're late.	**We'd** never gone there.	If I were you, **I'd** do it.

will	*not*
I'll be at home.	That **isn't** right.
You'll like the movie.	They **weren't** clean.
They'll be late.	She **won't** go.

Reductions

After nouns, many auxiliary verbs have reduced pronunciations. The vowel may be pronounced /ə/ and consonants may be simplified. The reduced verb joins closely to surrounding words. You should be familiar with how these reductions sound. If it's difficult for you to join words closely together, you can use the full verb forms after nouns, but don't stress them.

1. **Reduction of *are*.** When *are* follows a noun that ends in a consonant, it sounds like an *-er* ending and joins closely to the noun.

   Ships are large boats. ("shipser" large boats)

2. **Reductions of *is* and *has*.** When *is* or *has* follows a noun ending in /s, z, ʃ, ʒ, tʃ, dʒ/, it sounds like a long plural /əz/ and joins closely to the noun.

   The rose is red. (the "rosəz" red)

   Josh has gone home. ("joshəz" gone home)

3. **Reduction of *have*.** When *have* follows a noun that ends in a consonant, it sounds like *of* (/əv/) and joins closely to the noun.

   The ships have sailed. (the "shipsəv" sailed)

   The painters have finished. (the "paintersəv" finished)

4. **Reductions of *had* and *would*.** When *had* or *would* follows a noun that ends in a consonant, it's pronounced /əd/ and joins closely to the noun.

> Mark had better leave. ("markəd" better leave)
>
> Dad would like chicken. ("daddəd" like chicken)

5. **Reduction of *will*.** When *will* follows a noun that ends in a consonant, it's pronounced /əl/, like the last two letters in *local*. It joins closely to the noun.

> The bank will close early. (the "bankəl" close early)

STEP 2 FOCUSED PRACTICE

EXERCISE 1: Contractions

Listen and repeat the sentences. Use contractions.

1. I'm Íma.
2. You're Yúri.
3. They're thére.
4. He's Éaz.
5. We're wéird.
6. It's ítsy.
7. I'll álways trý.
8. We'd wéed the gárden if we cóuld.

EXERCISE 2: The Answer Machine

A | *Listen and fill in the blanks to complete the conversation.*

MARTY: Hi, Answer Machine. I'_____ doing my homework now, and

there'_____ some tough questions I _____ answer. Can you

help me out?

ANSWER MACHINE: Hi Marty. You'_____ tried hard to get the answers yourself, right?

MARTY: Of course, Answer Machine. You'_____ my last hope.

ANSWER MACHINE: OK, Marty. What'_____ the first question?

MARTY: Who invented the telephone?

ANSWER MACHINE: I'_____ check my data banks and let you know in an hour, OK?

B | *PAIRS: Compare your answers. Then practice the conversation.*

EXERCISE 3: U.S. Tourist Spots

A | *Listen to the questions and responses.*

Questions	Responses
_b_ **1.** Disney World's in Miami, isn't it?	**a.** No, it isn't. It's in Philadelphia.
____ **2.** The Statue of Liberty's in Washington, D.C., isn't it?	**b.** No, it isn't. It's in Orlando.
____ **3.** Fisherman's Wharf's in Los Angeles, isn't it?	**c.** No, it isn't. It's in Seattle.
	d. No, it isn't. It's in San Antonio.
____ **4.** The Liberty Bell's in Chicago, isn't it?	**e.** No, it isn't. It's in Cambridge.
	f. No, it isn't. It's in New Orleans.
____ **5.** Harvard's in Boston, isn't it?	**g.** No, it isn't. It's in Washington, D.C.
____ **6.** The Latin Quarter's in Seattle, isn't it?	**h.** No, it isn't. It's in Chicago.
____ **7.** The Sears Tower's in New York, isn't it?	**i.** No, it isn't. It's in San Francisco.
____ **8.** The Pentagon's in Baltimore, isn't it?	**j.** No, it isn't. It's in New York.
____ **9.** The Space Needle's in Phoenix, isn't it?	
____ **10.** The Alamo's in Houston, isn't it?	

B | *GROUPS: Match each question with its response. (You can check your answers on page 183.)*
Then read a question. Use rising intonation on the tag question, **isn't it?** *Choose a classmate to say the correct response.*

EXERCISE 4: Sounds Like . . .

A | *Two phrases that sound the same but have different spellings and meanings are called* homophrases. *Listen and repeat the phrases.*

1. Michael Wright   *Mike will write.*

2. Lunches Served Here _____

3. His cattle[1] drink water. _____

4. Rose's herd[2] _____

5. The waitresses quit serving. _____

6. The disinterested groan[3] _____

B | *PAIRS: Take turns saying each phrase. Then work with your partner to think of another phrase with a reduced or contracted verb that sounds the same (or nearly the same) and write it in the blank. (Hints: An* **-el** *or* **-le** *ending could be* will; *an* **-es** *ending could be* is *or* has; *an* **-ed** *ending could be* had *or* would.) *Practice saying each homophrase aloud. (Then check your answers on page 183.)*

STEP 3   COMMUNICATION PRACTICE

PREDICTIONS

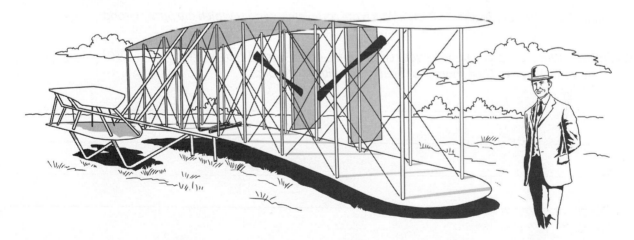

EXERCISE 5: Predicting the Future

In 1901, Wilbur Wright, co-inventor of the airplane, made a prediction: Man won't fly for 50 years. Two years later, Wilbur and his brother Orville made their first flight in a plane they'd built. By 1920, there were several commercial airlines around the world. People have always made predictions about the future. As the ones on the next page show, they aren't always right.

---

[1] cattle: *cows;* [2] herd: *a group of animals;* [3] groan: *a sound of displeasure*

A | *Listen to the predictions. Complete the sentences with* **will** *or* **won't**.

1. *1910.* By 1925, more electricity _____ be used for electric cars than for lights.

   Thomas Edison (inventor)

2. *1912.* The coming of the wireless age _____ make war impossible.

   Guglielmo Marconi (inventor of the radio)

3. *1966.* In the year 2000, shopping from home _____ be possible but it _____

   be popular. *Time Magazine*

4. *2004.* In two years, "spam"[1] _____ be a problem. *Bill Gates (cofounder of Microsoft)*

Natural English

Use the contraction *won't* when you speak. Uncontracted *will not* can sound like an order.

   Man *won't* fly for 50 years.

Pronounce *won't* and *want* differently. The vowel in *won't* is /ow/ (like the vowel in *go*). If your pronunciation of *won't* and *want* sound too similar, use the vowel in *father* when you say *want*.

   Man *won't want* to fly.

   People *won't want* to shop from home.

B | *PAIRS: Look at the predictions in Part A. Which are completely wrong? Which are partly wrong?*

C | *GROUPS: Write four predictions for your city, country, or the world. What will happen by 2050? What won't happen? Then share your predictions with your group.*

1. _____

2. _____

3. _____

4. _____

EXERCISE 6: The Reunion

A | *Jack Harper and Suzy Barolo have run into each other at their tenth year high school reunion. Listen to the conversation.*

JACK: Suzy? Suzy Barolo? It's Jack. Jack Harper. Do you remember me?

SUZY: Jack! How could I forget you? You look just the same—well, you have a little less hair.

JACK: Oh, yeah—and a few more pounds! But you're exactly the same. How are you? What've you been doing?

---

[1] spam: *unwanted email, often sent by advertisers using large lists of email addresses*

SUZY: Well, I've lived in Boise now for four years. I'm managing to support myself singing—some clubs and radio commercials. Nothing big yet. But I'm having a good time. What about you? What're you doing?

JACK: Well, Chris and I got married right after high school. We're living in Seattle. Chris's traveling now, so she couldn't be here. She's an event planner for the Mariners, and she travels a lot. . . .

SUZY: Sounds exciting.

JACK: Suzy! Is that Marta Simpson? She's lost a lot of weight. She looks great!

B | *What do you think your classmates will be doing 10 years from now? Write questions to ask your classmates in the left column of the chart. Use contractions. Then write predictions about your life in 10 years in the right column.*

Questions to Ask Your Classmates	Your Life in 10 Years
Do you think you'll be married?	Personal life: _____
_____	_____
_____	_____
_____	Job: _____
_____	_____
_____	Other: _____
_____	_____

C | *PAIRS: Take turns asking each other the questions you wrote. Use contractions in your answers.*

STEP 4 EXTENDED PRACTICE

Accuracy Practice *Listen again to Exercise 1 on page 179. Then record the sentences.*

Fluency Practice *Record a description of how you think your life will be 10 years from now. You can use information from the chart in Exercise 6B or add new information. Include sentences with **will** or **won't**, and use contractions.*

EXAMPLE:

In 10 years, I think I'll be married. I'll probably be living in New York City.

EXERCISE 3B: 1. b, 2. j, 3. i, 4. a, 5. e, 6. f, 7. h, 8. g, 9. c, 10. d
EXERCISE 4B: 1. Mike will write. 2. Lunch is served here. 3. His cat will drink water. 4. Rose is/has heard. 5. The waitress has quit serving. 6. The disinterest had grown.

Rhythm Patterns of Prepositions

STEP 1 PRESENTATION

Prepositions are unstressed in prepositional phrases (*at níght*). In phrasal verbs, the preposition is stressed (*come ín*).

Rhythm Patterns of Prepositions

1. **Prepositions in Prepositional Phrases**

    Short prepositions in prepositional phrases are not stressed.

    at níght   in a mínute   to schóol

    The vowel in some prepositions is reduced to /ə/. You'll understand English better if you're familiar with these reductions.

    at hóme   for a whíle   to the móvies
    /ət/   /fər/   /tə/

    Of is unstressed and pronounced /əv/. Before consonants, it's often pronounced /ə/ and joins closely to the surrounding words.

    a cup of coffee (a "cuppə" coffee)

    To is unstressed when it's a preposition (*to* the bank) or part of an infinitive (I like *to* dance). *To* is often pronounced with the full vowel /uw/ when the next word begins with an unstressed vowel. Before words beginning with consonants, *to* is pronounced /tə/.

    to enjóy   to dó
    /tuw/   /tə/

    Long prepositions with clear meaning can be stressed.

    agáinst the dóor   betwéen the cháirs   óver the híll

2. **Prepositions in Phrasal Verbs**

    When prepositions such as *on*, *in*, and *up* are used in phrasal verbs, they aren't reduced. The words in the verb phrase join closely together.

    Come ón.   Pick it úp.   Wake úp.

STEP 2 FOCUSED PRACTICE

EXERCISE 1: Prepositional Phrases

🎧 *Listen and repeat the phrases. Pronounce the words as one group. Don't stress the preposition.*

1. at hóme
2. at níght
3. at the gým
4. to schóol
5. to a réstaurant

6. from wórk
7. for cláss
8. for a yéar
9. with fríends
10. in México

11. in a mínute
12. in a húrry
13. on the wéekend
14. on a díet
15. óne of his idéas

EXERCISE 2: Hearing Prepositions

🎧 **A** | *Listen to the conversations. Write the prepositions you hear in the blanks.*

1. **A:** Let's meet _____ the gym.

   B: I'm not going _____ the gym today.

2. **A:** If you can wait _____ an hour, I can give you a ride

   _____ work.

   B: Thanks, but I need to be _____ work early today.

3. **A:** Can you come _____ me to the shoe store?

   B: Sure. I need to look _____ a new pair _____ boots.

4. **A:** Lucy's returning _____ Las Vegas today.

   B: Are you picking her up _____ the airport?

5. **A:** Let's meet _____ campus _____ an hour.

   B: OK. Will you be _____ the library?

6. **A:** I haven't eaten chocolate _____ three days.

   B: Are you _____ a diet?

B | *PAIRS: Compare your answers. Then practice the conversations.*

EXERCISE 3: Prepositional Phrases and Idioms

A | *Listen and repeat the phrases and idioms.*

at once	for good	in a jam	on a diet
at noon	for the time being	in a minute	on time

B | *Listen to the questions.*

1. What's an idiom that means "immediately"? _____

2. When is the sun directly overhead? _____

3. What do you say when you're trying to lose weight? *I'm* _____.

4. What's an idiom that means "permanently"? _____

5. What's an idiom that means "now but possibly not later"? _____

6. What's an idiom that means "in trouble"? _____

7. What's an idiom that means "not late"? _____

8. It's 3:00 now. When will it be 3:01 (three-oh-one)? _____

C | *PAIRS: Use the phrases and idioms from Part A to answer the questions. Write your answers on the lines in Part B. Then practice saying the questions and answers.*

EXERCISE 4: Phrasal Verbs

Listen and repeat the phrasal verbs. Stress the preposition and join words together.

1. finish up
2. come on
3. wake up
4. hand it in
5. clean it up
6. turned it on
7. throw it out
8. go in
9. figure it out
10. put it off
11. try it on
12. picked it up

EXERCISE 5: Using Idioms and Phrasal Verbs

A | *Complete the sentences with the idioms and phrasal verbs you hear.*

1. **A:** Are you still _____?

   B: Yes. So far I've lost 10 pounds.

   A: That's great!

   B: Yeah. I hope I can keep it off _____.

2. **A:** I'm _____— I got up late. Can you give me a ride to school?

   B: You have an alarm clock. Don't you ever _____?

   A: Yeah, but I always _____ and fall back asleep.

   B: OK. _____, let's go.

B | *PAIRS: Practice the conversations. Don't stress prepositions in prepositional phrases. Stress particles in phrasal verbs.*

STEP 3   COMMUNICATION PRACTICE

FOOD AND NUTRITION

EXERCISE 6: An Unusual Diet That Worked

A | *Complete the sentences with prepositions, articles, pronouns, conjunctions, or auxiliary verbs.*

Jared Fogle had weight problems. In college, _____ weighed 425 pounds (197.3 kg).
1.

_____ shoulders _____ knees hurt—even _____ wasn't moving. He
2.   3.   4.

knew he had _____ lose weight, but _____ first attempts failed. And then
5.   6.

he found a diet _____ worked—eating out* _____ a fast-food chain. He
                    7.   8.

decided _____ skip breakfast and eat only two meals a day, always at the fast food
                9.

restaurant and never _____ home. Jared went _____ consuming 10,000
                              10.   11.

calories _____ day to 2,000. Each meal included a low-calorie submarine sandwich,
              12.

some baked (not fried) potato chips, and either water _____ a diet soda. And he started
                                                            13.

walking _____ exercise.
                14.

One year later, Jared had lost 245 pounds (111.1 kg). His college newspaper wrote a story

about his unusual diet. The story came _____ the attention _____ fast food
                                                15.   16.

chain. The chain decided _____ make an ad featuring Jared, _____ "before"
                                  17.   18.

and "after" pictures. _____ the ad, Jared told the story _____ how he'd lost
                            19.   20.

weight by eating out at the fast food chain. After _____ success _____ the ad,
                                                          21.   22.

Jared became a celebrity.

---

*Natural English

The idiom *eat out* is a common way to say "go to a restaurant." Join the two words
closely together, and stress the word *out*.

Jared lost weight by always eating óut.

🎧 **B** | *Now listen to Part A and check your answers.*

C | *PAIRS: Answer the questions.*

1. Why do you think Jared's diet worked?
2. Do you think Jared could have lost the same amount of weight by going to a different fast
   food chain?
3. Could you eat the same thing, day after day, for a year?

EXERCISE 7: Your Turn

A | *What's important to you when you make food choices? Does your answer depend on where you're eating? Check (✓) the four most important factors in the chart below. Then add other factors to the bottom of the chart.*

Food Factors	Eating at Home	Eating Out
taste		
freshness		
convenience		
price		
nutrients		
calories		
natural		
unprocessed		
filling		
amount of salt		

B | *GROUPS: Compare your charts. Do you and your classmates agree on what factors are most important?*

STEP 4   EXTENDED PRACTICE

Accuracy Practice *Listen again to Exercises 1 and 4 on pages 185 and 186. Then record the phrases.*

Fluency Practice *Record your answers to the questions.*

1. What foods do you like to eat?
2. Do you think those foods are healthy choices? Why or why not?

Rising and Falling Intonation

STEP 1 PRESENTATION

Intonation is the melody of language, the pattern of high and low notes over phrases and sentences. Your intonation at the end of a sentence tells the listener how to respond to you.

I'm going to get married.

Intonation at the End of a Sentence

1. **Final rising intonation is used to show:**

   You aren't sure about something. Final rising intonation is common with *yes/no* questions.

   Do you have to work this weekend?   Are you hungry?

   You haven't finished speaking.

   I know . . . (The speaker hasn't finished speaking.)

   You didn't hear what a speaker said.

   A: I have some news.

   B: What?

   A: I said, I have some news.

2. **Final falling intonation is used to show:**

   You believe what you say is true. Final falling intonation is common with statements. Intonation falls after the highlighted word.

   There's a storm coming.

   You've finished speaking.

   I know.

   You need a specific piece of information. Final falling intonation is common with *wh-* questions.

   When is the concert? (The speaker knows there is a concert but doesn't know when.)

Intonation in Lists

Intonation usually rises on the first words in a list and falls on the last. The final fall tells the listener the list is finished. This intonation is common with phrases joined by *and* and *or*.

winter, spring, summer, and fall

EXERCISE 1: Minimal Conversations

A | *Minimal conversations are made of single words or short phrases. In minimal conversations, almost all the words are highlighted. Listen to the conversation. Draw intonation lines (⌣ or ⌢) to show the intonation.*

LIANG: Here? _____ ⌣ _____

MOHAMMED: There. _____

LIANG: Why? _____

MOHAMMED: Recycling rules. _____

            Glass here. _____. Plastic there. _____

LIANG: Paper? _____

MOHAMMED: There. _____

B | *PAIRS: Compare your answers. Then practice the conversation. Take turns.*

EXERCISE 2: One-Word Conversations

A | *PAIRS: Order each set of questions and answers to make a conversation. What are the conversations about?*

Conversation 1	Conversation 2	Write Your Own
_____ **A:** Again.	_____ **B:** Too bad.	**A:** _____
_1_ **B:** Snow?	_____ **B:** Beach?	**B:** _____
_____ **A:** Buried.	_____ **A:** Contamination.[1]	**A:** _____
_____ **B:** How much?	_____ **A:** Yeah.	**B:** _____
_____ **A:** A lot.	_____ **A:** Closed.	**A:** _____
_____ **B:** The car?	_____ **B:** Why?	**B:** _____

B | *Write your own minimal conversation in the right column of the chart in Part A.*

---

[1] contamination: *water, soil, or air pollution*

EXERCISE 3: Lists

A | *Listen to the lists. Pay attention to the intonation on the last word. Draw an intonation line over the last word in each list (⌣ or ⌒). If the speaker has finished the list, write **yes** in the blank. If the speaker hasn't finished, write **no**.*

		Finished?
1.	January, February, March⌒	yes
2.	one, two, three	_____
3.	air pollution, water pollution, soil pollution	_____
4.	who, what, where, why	_____
5.	plastic, metal, glass	_____
6.	reduce, reuse, recycle	_____
7.	third, fourth, fifth	_____
8.	Friday, Saturday, Sunday	_____

B | *PAIRS: Compare your answers. Then choose a list and say it aloud. Use rising or falling intonation on the last word. Your partner will tell you whether the list is finished or unfinished.*

EXERCISE 4: Rising and Falling Intonation

A | *Listen to the conversation.*

YOSHI: How was beachcombing?

SARA: What?

YOSHI: I said, "How was beachcombing?" You went beachcombing, right?

SARA: Oh yeah. It was disappointing. There was a lot of garbage—old shoes, plastic bags, water bottles. . . . But I found this shell.

YOSHI: What kind is it?

SARA: A conch shell.

B | *PAIRS: Practice the conversation. Follow the intonation lines. Take turns.*

IT'S GOOD FOR THE PLANET

EXERCISE 5: A New Place to Eat

A | *Listen and repeat the conversation. Follow the intonation lines over the questions.*

RAY: Have you ever been to Daley's?

SUSANA: Yes. It's good, but I'd like to go somewhere new.

           How about the College Inn? Have you ever been there?

RAY: No, but I think it's vegetarian. What about Michael's?

           It's a new seafood restaurant. Have you ever eaten there?

SUSANA: No. That's another possibility.

RAY: So, what do you feel like?

SUSANA: Vegetarian. It's good for the planet.

RAY: Vegetarian? But what about my stomach?

SUSANA: Vegetarian is also good for your stomach.

Natural English

Use *How about . . .* and *What about . . .* to make informal suggestions
or to suggest alternatives.

How about the College Inn?

What about Michael's?

B | *PAIRS: Practice the conversation. Take turns.*

EXERCISE 6: Your Turn

A | *Read about how a town in New York tried to reduce its impact on the environment.*

In January 2011, the small town of Stone Ridge, New York, asked its residents to reduce their harmful impact on the environment by taking part in a "No Impact" Week. Stone Ridge had a seven-day plan. On the first day, residents bought fewer things. This reduced trash, since a large amount of what we buy ends up in the garbage within six months. On the second day, residents tried not to waste anything. For example, they reused paper with writing on only one side. On the third day, residents tried to use their cars less and walk to places instead. On the fourth day, the town asked residents to eat only locally produced food. The organizers explained that the average product in a grocery store travels 1,500 miles (2,414 km). As a result, it requires more fuel than locally grown food. On the fifth day, residents tried to reduce their use of electricity by turning off computers or lights when they weren't in use. On the sixth day, residents used less water by taking shorter showers and fixing leaky faucets. During the first six days, residents limited their negative impact on the environment. On the last day, they made a positive impact on the town by performing community services.

B | *Write three specific things you could do to reduce your electricity use, garbage, and water use.*

Reduce Electricity Use	Reduce Garbage	Reduce Water Use
1.	1.	1.
2.	2.	2.
3.	3.	3.

C | *GROUPS: Share the information from your chart with your classmates. Use listing intonation when you can.*

D | *GROUPS: Read the information below and then answer the question.*

The No Impact Movement believes that individuals can do a lot to improve the environment. The Movement often criticizes governments for moving too slowly to solve environmental problems. Do you agree or disagree with the Movement—can individual efforts make a big difference? Explain.

STEP 4 EXTENDED PRACTICE

Accuracy Practice *Listen again to Exercise 1A on page 191. Then record the conversation.*

Fluency Practice *Record your answers to the questions.*

1. What do you do to protect the environment?
2. Do you think people do enough to protect the environment? Explain.

Other Uses of Intonation

STEP 1 PRESENTATION

Choice questions are pronounced with both rising and falling intonation. Rising intonation is also used to check understanding and agreement and to ask for repetitions.

Choice Questions

Intonation rises on the first choice and falls on the second. The choices are usually joined with *or*.

Are you going to study or go out?

Checking Understanding and Agreement

Check understanding by adding *right*, with rising intonation.

You're going to be home by 10:00, right?

Check agreement by adding *OK*, with rising intonation.

Let's go, OK?

Asking for Repetitions

You can use these questions to ask someone to repeat:

Could you repeat that?

Can you repeat that?

What?

What did you say?

When you use a *wh-* question to ask for information, use falling intonation.

I finally talked to the teacher about my test.

What did you say?

I told her the truth. I don't understand the grammar and I need extra work.

(continued on next page)

Giving Yourself Time: Let's see . . .

You can say "Let's see . . .", with a level tone, to give yourself time to think.

A: I couldn't find the news story you told me about last night. Where did you hear it?

B: Let's see . . . I think it was on CNN. Did you check their website?

Parentheticals

Parentheticals are phrases such as *I think* and *I guess* added to the end of a sentence. They're pronounced with low intonation. Low intonation tells the listener that the parenthetical phrase isn't part of the main sentence. At the end of the parenthetical, intonation may rise a little.

The news story was on CNN, I think.

STEP 2 FOCUSED PRACTICE

EXERCISE 1: Choice Questions and Parentheticals

A | *Listen to the conversations.*

1. **A:** Is the test on Monday or Tuesday?

   B: Let's see . . . Monday, I think.

2. **A:** It's getting late.

   B: We should go home, I guess.

3. **A:** There's a 50 percent chance of snow tomorrow. I don't know whether I should drive or take the bus.

   B: Take the bus. If it snows, traffic will be terrible.

4. **A:** Is Lucy's new husband an actor or a singer?

   B: An actor, I heard.

B | *PAIRS: Practice the conversations. Take turns.*

EXERCISE 2: Asking for a Repetition or Information

A | *Listen and repeat the conversations. Notice the intonation on the question words.*

1. **A:** I have something to tell you.

   B: What?

   A: I said I have something to tell you.

2. **A:** I have something to tell you.

   B: What?

   A: Lucy got married in Las Vegas!

B | *PAIRS: Complete the conversations below. Student B should choose rising or falling intonation for the question word. Rising intonation means that Student B wants a repetition. Falling intonation means that Student B wants more information. Student A should answer Student B's question by repeating information or adding information that answers Student B's question.*

1. **A:** I have some bad news.

   B: What?

   A: _____

2. **A:** I saw something strange on my way to work today.

   B: What?

   A: _____

EXERCISE 3: Checking Understanding: *Right?*

A | *Listen to the conversation.*

ANA: Lucy got married, right?

SAM: That's right. In Las Vegas.

ANA: You met her husband. What's he like?

SAM: I don't really know. She just introduced him to me.

ANA: But he's an actor, right? Is he good-looking?

SAM: He's okay, I guess. I don't know whether he's an actor or wants to be an actor.

ANA: I wonder if we should get her a wedding present.

SAM: I don't know. You only have to give a present if you're invited to the wedding, right?

B | *PAIRS: Practice the conversation. Do you think Ana and Sam need to buy a wedding present for Lucy and Max?*

PARENTS AND CHILDREN

EXERCISE 4: Breaking the News

A | Listen to the conversation.

MRS. BEVINS:	Harry, that was Lucy on the phone.
MR. BEVINS:	Mmm-hmm.* How is she?
MRS. BEVINS:	Married.
MR. BEVINS:	That's nice.
MRS. BEVINS:	Harry, put down your newspaper! I said, Lucy's married.
MR. BEVINS:	Married? Who did she marry? When?
MRS. BEVINS:	Oh, Harry, I don't know. She said he wants to be an actor. They got married in Las Vegas last night.
MR. BEVINS:	In Las Vegas? An actor? He's not an Elvis impersonator, is he?

---

*Natural English

In conversations, you can say, "Mmm-hmm" or "Uh-huh," to let someone know you're paying attention (even if you really aren't).

MRS. BEVINS:	Harry, that was Lucy on the phone.
MR. BEVINS:	Mmm-hmm. How is she?

B | PAIRS: Practice the conversation. Take turns.

EXERCISE 5: Meeting the In-Laws

Lucy and Max met each other in Las Vegas. They fell in love and got married the next night at the Tru Luv Chapel. On their way back to their new home in Los Angeles, they stopped for a day in San Francisco so Max could meet Lucy's parents. When they got back to Los Angeles, Lucy emailed her father.

A | *Listen to the email Lucy sent her father after their visit.*

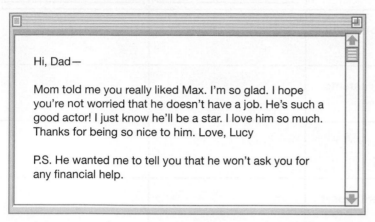

Hi, Dad—

Mom told me you really liked Max. I'm so glad. I hope you're not worried that he doesn't have a job. He's such a good actor! I just know he'll be a star. I love him so much. Thanks for being so nice to him. Love, Lucy

P.S. He wanted me to tell you that he won't ask you for any financial help.

B | *Listen to the response Lucy's father sent to her.*

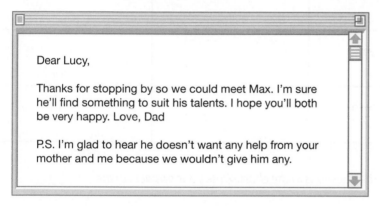

Dear Lucy,

Thanks for stopping by so we could meet Max. I'm sure he'll find something to suit his talents. I hope you'll both be very happy. Love, Dad

P.S. I'm glad to hear he doesn't want any help from your mother and me because we wouldn't give him any.

C | *PAIRS: Answer the questions.*

1. How does Lucy feel about Max? How does she think the visit with her parents went?
2. How does Lucy's father feel about Max?

EXERCISE 6: Your Turn

A | *Listen to the questions in the chart. Notice the intonation on the choice questions (questions with* or*). Then write your answers.*

	Your Name:	**Partner's Name:**
If Lucy's story were your story, how would your parents react?		
When you were growing up, were your parents strict or lenient?[1]		
After school, did you have to go home or could you hang out with your friends?		
If you got a bad grade, were your parents upset or forgiving?		
Did your parents help you when you didn't understand your homework?		
On school nights, did your parents let you watch TV? If so, how much?		
On weekends, could you go out alone with friends (without an adult)?		

B | *PAIRS: Take turns asking and answering the questions in the chart. Write your answers in the correct columns.*

STEP 4 EXTENDED PRACTICE

Accuracy Practice *Listen again to Exercise 1A on page 196. Then record the conversations.*

Fluency Practice *Record your answer to the question.*

Do you feel your parents were too strict, too lenient, or just right when you were growing up? Explain. Use parentheticals like *I think* or *I guess* if you're not sure.

---

[1] lenient: *not strict*

APPENDICES

1 FOR TEAM A PLAYERS / STUDENT A

UNIT 1

Exercise 5, page 4

Choose one of the words in parentheses and read the sentence to your partner. Your partner will write what you say.

1. Look at the (ship/sheep) in the picture.
2. How do you spell ("pull"/"pool")?
3. Get some (paper/pepper) at the store.

UNIT 6

Exercise 6B, page 30

Year	What Happened
1962	Frane Selak was riding on a train. Suddenly, the train left the rails and fell into an icy river. Seventeen people on the train died. Selak only broke his arm.
1963	
1966	Selak was riding on a bus. The bus drove off the road and into a river. Four people were killed, but Selak wasn't hurt.
1970	
1973	Selak was driving a car. Suddenly, fire began coming from the engine into the car. All of Selak's hair burned off, but he had no other injuries.

1995	
1996	Selak drove a car off a cliff to avoid crashing into a truck. Selak was thrown from the car and landed in a tree. The car exploded when it hit the ground.
2003	
Moral of the story (1)	Selak should stay away from mass transportation.
Moral of the story (2)	

UNIT 8

Exercise 6, page 39

1. What's the past tense of "hear"?
2. Where do you go to buy things?
3. What's the opposite of "finish"?
4. What's the opposite of "play"?
5. When two countries fight each other, there is _____.
6. What do people drive?
7. What's another word for "difficult"?
8. You enter a room through this opening.
9. What number follows 29?

Answers:

1. heard
2. (to a) store/(to) stores
3. start
4. work
5. war
6. cars
7. hard
8. (a) door
9. 30 (thirty)

UNIT 11

Exercise 4, page 56

Ask your partner: What's in box A2?

	1	2	3	4
A	peace			raise
B	gum	peas		
C	back		race	
D	bag		come	

UNIT 13

Exercise 4, page 67

1. listen
2. love
3. expect
4. need
5. play
6. drop
7. answer
8. fix
9. seem
10. arrest

Answers:

1. listened ("listend")
2. loved ("lovd")
3. expected (-*ed* is a syllable)
4. needed (-*ed* is a syllable)
5. played ("playd")
6. dropped ("dropt")
7. answered ("answerd")
8. fixed ("fikst")
9. seemed ("seemd")
10. arrested (-*ed* is a syllable)

UNIT 14

Exercise 4, page 72

1. What's an unlucky number?
2. What's 10 x 3 (ten times three)?
3. What's the opposite of "unhealthy"?
4. How do you pronounce T-H-O-R-O-U-G-H?
5. If you're in California and you want to go to Washington State, do you go north or south?
6. What's the opposite of "fat"?
7. How much is 10 + 3 (ten plus three)?
8. On your hand you have four fingers and one _____.
9. What should you say when someone does something nice for you?
10. Is Mexico north or south of Canada?
11. Your parents include your _____ and your _____.

Answers:

1. thirteen
2. thirty
3. healthy
4. thorough [θərow]
5. north
6. thin
7. thirteen
8. thumb
9. thank you (or thanks)
10. south
11. mother, father

UNIT 15

Exercise 6, page 78

1. What's the name of the sixth letter of the alphabet?
2. What's the general name for foods, such as apples, pears, cherries, and strawberries?
3. What's the opposite of "sad"?
4. What's the name of the sport where tall people throw balls through a hoop?
5. Some people speak Spanish; some people speak English; some people speak Korean. Spanish, English, and Korean are _____.
6. What's the opposite of "hate"?
7. What's 50 + 5 (fifty plus five)?
8. What color do you get when you mix red and white together?
9. What's the opposite of "enemy"?
10. What's the superlative of "good"?
11. What number comes after 10?
12. What's the opposite of "small"?

Answers:

1. F /ɛf/
2. fruit
3. happy
4. basketball
5. languages
6. love
7. fifty-five
8. pink
9. friend
10. best
11. eleven
12. big

UNIT 16

Exercise 4, page 83

Ask your partner: What's in box A1?

	1	2	3	4
A		bus		buzzes
B	lacy	lazy		buzz
C			place	plays
D		places		

Exercise 7B, page 85

Situation	Lesson Learned
Bill Gates played sports as a child, but he wasn't very good at it. Gates wanted to quit, but his parents advised him to continue playing.	
The Gates' family ate meals together and talked about what they did each day.	
Gates took computer classes in high school. Sometimes he fixed the computers when there were problems with them.	
Gates and Warren Buffet became friends. Buffet lives a simple life and always treats people with respect.	

UNIT 17

Exercise 5B, page 90

Country	Minimum paid vacation days	Paid public holidays
France		10
Hungary	23 (if over 31 years old)	
India		19
Italy	20	
Japan		15
Latvia	20	
Lebanon		18
Philippines	5	
South Africa		12
South Korea	19	
Thailand		13
United Arab Emirates	30	

UNIT 18

Exercise 3, page 93

Ask your partner: What's in box A2?

	1	2	3	4
A	catch		cash	
B	cheap	jeep		
C				joke
D		choice	choke	Joyce

Exercise 5, page 136

Ask your partner: What's in box A2?

	1	2	3	4
A	White House			white house
B	message	massage		
C	a dessert			
D		a desert	decent	descent

UNIT 28

Exercise 6, page 148

1. Ask Student B four questions about the dates in parentheses. Pronounce the date carefully. Use this question:

   What happened in _____?

   (1917, 1970, 1918, 1980)

2. Answer Student B's questions with this information:

   1914: World War I started.

   1940: Franklin Roosevelt was elected president for the third time.

   1916: Woodrow Wilson was elected president.

   1960: JFK was elected president.

UNIT 33

Exercise 6B, page 176

When you are the job counselor, read these sentences to your partner.

This company needs someone who can teach ballroom dancing.

This company needs someone who can greet the public and talk easily with strangers.

This company needs someone who can speak French fluently.

This company needs someone who can develop business software.

UNIT 1

Exercise 5, page 4

Choose one of the words in parentheses and read the sentence to your partner. Your partner will write what you say.

1. Is that a picture of a (cop/cup)?
2. I want to (live/leave) quietly.
3. I have a (pain/pen) in my hand.

UNIT 6

Exercise 6B, page 30

Year	What Happened
1962	
1963	Frane Selak was flying on a plane. Suddenly the door of the plane blew off. Selak fell out of the plane and landed in a haystack. His only injuries were cuts and bruises.
1966	
1970	Selak was driving a car. The car began to have trouble. Selak jumped out of the car just before it exploded. Selak wasn't hurt.
1973	
1995	Selak was hit by a bus, but he was not hurt.
1996	
2003	Selak bought the first lottery ticket of his life. He won a million dollars.
Moral of the story (1)	
Moral of the story (2)	Selak should not drive.

UNIT 8

Exercise 6, page 39

1. This is in your body. It pumps blood.
2. What do you stand on inside a building?
3. In baseball, what base comes after second base?
4. What's the name of the day you were born?
5. What's another word for "big"?
6. What's the opposite of "near"?
7. What animals fly?
8. What's the opposite of "less"?
9. What do you find in dictionaries?

Answers:

1. (the/your) heart	4. birthday	7. birds
2. (the) floor	5. large	8. more
3. third (base)	6. far	9. words

UNIT 11

Exercise 4, page 56

Ask your partner: What's in box A1?

	1	2	3	4
A		rice	rise	
B			have	pie
C		cap		cab
D		buy		half

UNIT 13

Exercise 4, page 67

1. open
2. walk (the *l* is silent: *walk*)
3. help
4. suggest
5. count
6. move
7. change
8. like
9. practice
10. die

Answers:

1. opened ("opend")
2. walked ("walkt")
3. helped ("helpt")
4. suggested (*-ed* is a syllable)
5. counted (*-ed* is a syllable)
6. moved ("movd")
7. changed ("changd")
8. liked ("likt")
9. practiced ("practist")
10. died

UNIT 14

Exercise 4, page 72

1. Is Miami north or south of New York City?
2. What do you call the top part of the leg, above the knee?
3. The word "dead" is an adjective. What is the noun?
4. How much is 1,000 x 3 (one thousand times three)?
5. What's the name of the day after Wednesday?
6. If you're in New York and you want to go to Florida, do you go north or south?
7. How much is 12 + 1 (twelve plus one)?
8. What is the plural of "this"?
9. How do you pronounce T-H-O-U-G-H?
10. Where can you see a movie or a play?
11. Your mother's son is your _____.

Answers:

1. south
2. the thigh
3. death
4. three thousand
5. Thursday
6. south
7. thirteen
8. these
9. though [ðow]
10. (in/at a) theater
11. brother

UNIT 15

Exercise 6, page 78

1. What's a common plural word used to refer to human beings?
2. What's 5 x 5 (five times five)?
3. You kiss with your _____.
4. What do people do in elections?
5. What's a word that means "not ever"?
6. Two common spices are salt and _____.
7. These animals swim and live in water.
8. What's a synonym for "start"?
9. What's the opposite of "rude"?
10. What do the words *windy, rainy, sunny,* and *cloudy* describe?
11. These sea animals are the largest animals on Earth.
12. You have these on your hands.

Answers:

1. people
2. twenty-five
3. lips
4. vote
5. never
6. pepper
7. fish (or whales, dolphins, octopi, etc.)
8. begin
9. polite
10. weather
11. whales
12. fingers

UNIT 16

Exercise 4, page 83

Ask your partner: What's in box A2?

	1	2	3	4
A	loose		buses	
B			loses	
C	price	lose		
D	prize		rice	rise

Exercise 7B, page 85

Situation	Lesson Learned
	Gates learned to try new things.
	Gates learned to talk to adults. He also learned about his parents' business dealings and volunteer work.
	Gates learned how to lead a project. The experience also let him dream about how computers could develop in the future.
	When life gets difficult, Gates tries to focus on the important things in his life.

UNIT 17

Exercise 5B, page 90

Country	Minimum paid vacation days	Paid public holidays
France	30	
Hungary		10
India	12	
Italy		11
Japan	20	
Latvia		11
Lebanon	15	
Philippines		14
South Africa	21	
South Korea		11
Thailand	6	
United Arab Emirates		9

UNIT 18

Exercise 3, page 93

Ask your partner: What's in box A1?

	1	2	3	4
A		Ed's		edge
B			H	age
C	watch	mush	much	
D	wash			

UNIT 26

Exercise 5, page 136

Ask your partner: What's in box A1?

	1	2	3	4
A		blackboard	black board	
B			really	rely
C		mystic	darkroom	mistake
D	dark room			

UNIT 28

Exercise 6, page 148

1. Answer Student A's questions with this information:

   1917: JFK was born.

   1970: There were violent demonstrations in the United States against the Vietnam War.

   1918: World War I ended.

   1980: Ronald Reagan was elected president.

2. Ask Student A four questions about the dates in parentheses. Pronounce the dates carefully. Use this question:

   What happened in _____?

   (1914, 1940, 1916, 1960)

Exercise 6B, page 176

When you are the job counselor, read these sentences to your partner.

This company needs someone who can work independently, without supervision.

This company needs someone who can work well with others, on a team.

This company needs someone who can speak Spanish fluently.

This company needs someone who can drive.

Windows XP Operating System

Recording

1. Plug in the microphone.

2. Open the START menu and click on the following: ALL PROGRAMS → ACCESSORIES → ENTERTAINMENT → SOUND RECORDER.

3. With the microphone plugged into the computer, click the red RECORD button and speak into the microphone. The recorder will record one minute of speech. Click the red RECORD button again to continue recording.

Saving and Compressing

4. Open the FILE menu and click SAVE AS. Compress the file if it is large: On the SAVE AS window, click the CHANGE button. In the SOUND SELECTION window, under FORMAT, select MPegLayer 3 (MP3). Close the SOUND SELECTION window. Name the file and save it.

Sending

5. The file can now be attached to an email and sent.

Windows VISTA and Windows 7 Operating System

Recording and Saving

1. Plug in the microphone.

2. Open the START menu and click on the following: ALL PROGRAMS → ACCESSORIES → SOUND RECORDER.

3. Click the red START RECORDING button and speak into the microphone.

4. Click the STOP RECORDING button when you finish. A SAVE box will appear. Name the file and save it.

Compressing and Sending

5. Right click on the saved sound file. SEND TO → COMPRESSED (ZIPPED)

6. Attach the compressed file to an email and send it.

MACINTOSH

Recording and Saving

1. Open an existing Sound Recording application on your Mac. If you do not have a Sound Recording application installed, download and install the free version of **Audacity**™ sound recorder (http://audacity.sourceforge.net/download/). It is very easy to use.

2. After installing **Audacity**™, open the application from your desktop and then use the recording tools to Record, Stop, Rewind, Pause, or Fast-forward.

3. To save the recorded file, click on the FILE menu and then click on EXPORT AS MP3.

4. Choose the location to save the file and then click on SAVE.

STUDENT AUDIO CD-ROM TRACKING GUIDE

The Student Audio CD-ROM has MP3 files for these Accuracy Practice exercises.